■SCHOLASTIC

50
LITERACY HOURS FOR
LESS ABLE
LEARNERS

- Tricky topics covered
- Shared texts for a lower reading age
- Photocopiable activities

AGES 7-9

Julie Coyne

CREDITS ■

Author	**Illustrations**
Julie Coyne	Edward Eaves
Editor	**Series Designer**
Victoria Lee	Anna Oliwa
Assistant Editor	**Designer**
Jane Gartside	Erik Ivens

Text © Julie Coyne
© 2005 Scholastic Ltd

Designed using Adobe InDesign

Published by Scholastic Ltd
Villiers House
Clarendon Avenue
Leamington Spa
Warwickshire CV32 5PR

www.scholastic.co.uk

Printed by Bell & Bain

4 5 6 7 8 9 0   6 7 8 9 0 1 2 3 4

British Library Cataloguing-in-Publication Data
A catalogue record for this book is available from the British Library.

ISBN 0-439-97178-0
ISBN 978-0439-97178-0

The right of Julie Coyne to be identified as the author of this work has been asserted by her in accordance with the Copyright, Designs and Patents Act 1988.

Extracts from The National Literacy Strategy © Crown copyright. Reproduced under the terms of HMSO Guidance Note 8.

ACKNOWLEDGEMENTS ■

The publishers gratefully acknowledge permission to reproduce the following copyright material: **James Carter** for 'Dennis' by James Carter from *The Works* edited by Paul Cookson ©2000, James Carter (2000, Macmillan). **Laura Cecil Literary Agency** on behalf of the Estate of James Reeves for 'The Magic Seeds' from *Complete Poems for Children* by James Reeves © James Reeves (Classic Mammoth) and 'The Froggy Princess' by Nicholas Fisk from *Pob's Stories* edited by Anne Wood ©1986, Nicholas Fisk (1986, Young Lions). **Anita Ganeri** for 'How Valleys Form' from *Factfinders: The Natural World* by Anita Ganeri and Moira Butterfield ©1990, Anita Ganeri (1990, Victoria House). **David Higham Associates** for extracts from *It's not fair* by Bel Mooney ©1989, Bel Mooney (1989, Methuen) and *I can't find it* by Bel Mooney ©1989, Bel Mooney (1989, Mammoth); for the poem 'There are Big Waves' by Eleanor Farjeon from *Silver, Sand and Snow* by Eleanor Farjeon ©1951, Eleanor Farjeon (1951, Michael Joseph); for an extract from *Fantastic Mr Fox* by Roald Dahl ©1968, Roald Dahl (1968, Allen & Unwin) and for an extract from *George's Marvellous Medicine* by Roald Dahl ©1981, Roald Dahl (1981, Bodley Head). **Tony Mitton** for 'Undersea Tea' by Tony Mitton from *The Works* edited by Paul Cookson © 2000, Tony Mitton (2000, Macmillan). **New Directions Publishing Corporation** for 'Spring Rain' by Tu Fu, translated by Kenneth Rexroth from *Collected Shorter Poems* ©1956, New Directions Publishing Corporation. (1956, New Directions Publishing Corp.). **The Penguin Group (UK)** for an extract from *George Speaks* by Dick King-Smith ©1988, Dick King-Smith (1988, Kestrel) and an extract from *The Worst Witch* by Jill Murphy ©1974, Jill Murphy (1978, Puffin). **Campbell Perry** for 'Writing Plays: The Wrong Bag' ©2005, Campbell Perry, previously unpublished. **The Random House Group** for an extract from *The Suitcase Kid* by Jacqueline Wilson ©1992, Jacqueline Wilson (1992, Corgi Yearling). **Irene Rawnsley** for 'True Confession' by Irene Rawnsley from *Fun with Poems* edited by Irene Yates ©2000, Irene Rawnsley (2000, Brilliant Publications). **Rogers, Coleridge and White Ltd** for two extracts from *Grace and Family* by Mary Hoffman ©1995, Mary Hoffman (1995, Frances Lincoln). **Coral Rumble** for 'Cats Can' by Coral Rumble from *The Works* edited by Paul Cookson ©2000, Coral Rumble (2000, Macmillan). **Scholastic Limited** for 'Writing Instructions' by Neela Mann and 'Hey you! Yes you!' by Neela Mann ©2005, Scholastic Limited, previously unpublished. **The Arthur Waley Estate** for 'After Rain' by Arthur Waley from *Bull's Eyes* edited by Brian Thompson ©1977, Arthur Waley (1977, Longman). **Walker Books Limited** for 'The Shape I'm In' by James Carter from *Cars, Stars, Electric Guitars* by James Carter ©2002, James Carter (2002, Walker Books) and for an extract from *Panda - Animals at Risk Series* by Judy Allen ©1992, Judy Allen (1992, Walker Books). **The Watts Publishing Group** for an extract from 'Freedom for Prometheus' from *The Orchard Book of Greek Myths* by Geraldine McCaughrean ©1992, Geraldine McCaughrean (1992, Orchard Books).

Contents

50 LITERACY HOURS
FOR LESS ABLE LEARNERS AGES 7 TO 9

This series of three books provides a range of activities with the less able learners in any classroom in mind. The activities cover many of the main objectives in the National Literacy Strategy at word, sentence and text level.

Each lesson uses photocopiable games, activities and examples designed to help the slower learner understand and develop and expand their literacy when reading, writing, speaking and listening. The lesson plans are designed to:
● enable teachers to explain word- and sentence-level work in a simple, step-by-step approach
● guide the writing process by giving the teacher suggestions to model and ideas for sharing and planning in relation to text-level work
● motivate the children with engaging activities and games
● address different learning styles and levels by providing a variety of activities.

About the book
Each book is made up of 50 lesson plans with an accompanying photocopiable activity and, in order to make the book simple to use, the lessons all follow a similar pattern. At the back of the book are photocopiable text extracts that can be used to address the text-level criteria, providing the teacher with good examples from children's literature as and when it is needed.

How to use this book
Each lesson is written to address one or two specific NLS objectives from Years 3 and 4 and these are given at the start of each lesson plan. The objectives grid at the beginning of the book shows tracking back, if the subject area has already been introduced in Years 1 or 2.

These lessons will help you to teach literacy in a creative and inspiring way. The activities are designed for practising and reinforcing the learning from the beginning part of the lesson. The independent activities, usually produced as photocopiable sheets, are presented in a variety of formats to try to accommodate a range of learning styles, and the children should be encouraged to work with as little adult support as possible.

The 'Plenary' may be a brief assessment and review, a few more turns of a game or a quick variation on the main activity. The lessons and accompanying photocopiable activities are written as stand-alone units and can be used by the teacher or teaching assistant at any point in the school year. The activities are designed to fit into the individual teacher's planning for literacy.

Title of lesson	Y4 Objectives	Y3 Objectives or tracking back	Y2	Y1
Long vowel phonemes	**T2 & 3. W1:** To identify phonemes in speech and writing; blend phonemes for reading and segment words into phonemes for spelling.	**T1–3. W1:** To revise and consolidate the spelling of words containing each of the long vowel phonemes from KS1 (Appendix List 3). **T2 & 3. W2:** To identify phonemes in speech and writing; blend phonemes for reading and segment words into phonemes for spelling.	T1–3. W1.	T3. W1.
Word families	**T2 & 3. W1:** To identify phonemes in speech and writing; blend phonemes for reading and segment words into phonemes for spelling.	**T1–3. W1:** To revise and consolidate the spelling of words containing each of the long vowel phonemes from KS1 (Appendix List 3). **T2 & 3. W2:** To identify phonemes in speech and writing; blend phonemes for reading and segment words into phonemes for spelling.	T1–3. W1.	T3. W1.
Happy word families	**T2 & 3. W1:** To identify phonemes in speech and writing; blend phonemes for reading and segment words into phonemes for spelling.	**T1–3. W1:** To revise and consolidate the spelling of words containing each of the long vowel phonemes from KS1 (Appendix List 3). **T2 & 3. W2:** To identify phonemes in speech and writing; blend phonemes for reading and segment words into phonemes for spelling.	T1–3. W1.	T3. W1.
Double consonant jumble	**T1. W5:** To spell two-syllable words containing double consonants.			
Alphabetical order	**T1. W12:** To use 3rd and 4th place letters to locate and sequence words in alphabetical order.	**T2. W23:** To organise words or information alphabetically, using the first two letters.	T2. T20.	T2. T20.
Capital letters and full stops		**T1. S11:** To write in complete sentences. **T1. S12:** To demarcate the end of a sentence with a full stop and the start of a new one with a capital letter.	T3. S5.	T1. S5, 8 & 9. T2. S4–7.
More capitalisation		**T2. S8:** To use capitalisation from reading, for example names, headings, special emphasis.	T1. S5.	T3. S5.
Remember verbs?	**T1. S2:** To investigate verb tenses (past, present and future).	**T1. S3:** To explore the function of verbs in sentences. **T1. S5:** To use the term 'verb' appropriately.	T1. W7. T2. S5. T3. S3.	T3. W6.
Past, present and future		**T1. S4:** To use verb tenses with increasing accuracy in speaking and writing. **T1. S5:** To use the term 'verb' appropriately.	T1. W7. T2. S5. T3. S3.	T3. W6.
Irregular verbs	**T1. W8:** To spell irregular tense changes.		T2. S5. T3. S3.	
Powerful verbs	**T1. S3:** To identify the use of powerful verbs.	**T1. S3:** To experiment changing simple verbs in sentences.		
Question or exclamation?	**T3. S3:** To understand how the grammar of a sentence alters when the sentence type is altered, when, for example a statement is made into a question.	**T1. S6:** To secure knowledge of question marks and exclamation marks in reading, understand their purpose and use appropriately in own writing.	T1. S3. T3. S6 & 7.	T3. S7.
Speech bubbles		**T1. S9:** To notice and investigate other devices for presenting texts, for example speech bubbles.	T2. S7.	
Speech marks		**T1. S7:** To secure the knowledge of basic conventions of speech punctuation. **T1. S8:** To use the term 'speech marks'.	T2. S6.	
Commas in lists		**T1. S13:** To use commas to separate items in a list.	T2. S8. T3. S4.	
Other comma uses	**T1. S5:** To practise using commas to mark grammatical boundaries within sentences.	**T2. S7:** To use the term 'comma' appropriately in relation to reading. **T3. S7:** To become aware of the use of commas in marking grammatical boundaries within sentences.	T1. S3.	

Title of lesson	Y4 objective(s)	Y3 objective(s)/tracking back	Y2	Y1
What is an adjective?		**T2. S2:** To identify and explore the function of adjectives within sentences. **T2. S3:** To use the term 'adjective' appropriately.		
Powerful adjectives	**T2. S1:** To revise and extend work on adjectives from Year 3, Term 2 and work on expressive and figurative language.	**T3. T2:** To refer to significant aspects of text, eg opening, build-up, atmosphere, and to know language is used to create these, eg use of adjectives for description.		
Singular or plural?		**T2. S4:** To extend knowledge and understanding of pluralisation. **T2. W11 & S5:** To use the terms 'singular' and 'plural' appropriately.	T1. W7.	T2. W8.
Collective nouns		**T2. S4:** To understand the term 'collective noun' and collecting examples – experiment with inventing other collective nouns.		
What is a pronoun?		**T3. S2:** To identify pronouns and understand their functions in sentences.	T2. S4. T3. S2.	
Conjunctions and connectives	**T2. T20:** To use connectives of time.	**T3. S5:** To explore how sentences can be joined in more complex ways by using a widening range of conjunctions.	T1. S2.	T3. T18.
Prefixes		**T1. W10:** To recognise and spell common prefixes and understand how these influence word meanings. **T1. W12:** To use the term 'prefix'.	T2. W8.	
Suffixes		**T2. W13:** To recognise and spell common suffixes and how these influence word meanings. **T2. W16:** To use the term 'suffix'.	T3. W7.	
What is an adverb?	**T1. S4:** To identify adverbs and understand their functions in sentences.			
Familiar setting		**T1. T1:** To compare a range of story settings, and to select words and phrases that describe scenes. **T1. T11:** To develop the use of settings in own stories.	T2. T5 & 13.	T1. T5 & 9. T3. T14.
Fantasy setting	**T2. T1:** To understand how writers create imaginary worlds.	**T1. T11:** To develop the use of settings in own stories		T3. T8.
Setting in a different culture	**T3. T2:** To read stories from other cultures.	**T1. T11:** To develop the use of settings in own stories.		
Myths, fables and traditional tales		**T2. T9:** To write a story plan for own myth, fable or traditional tale.		
Sequencing		**T3. T1:** To retell main points of a story in sequence.	T1. T4.	T2. T4. T3. T5.
Building atmosphere	**T2. T4:** To understand how the use of expressive and descriptive language can create mood, arouse expectations, build tension and so on.			
The passing of time	**T1. T3:** To explore chronology in narrative.		T1. T4 & 11.	
A character sketch	**T1. T11:** To write character sketches, focusing on small details to evoke sympathy or dislike.	**T2. T8:** To write portraits of characters.	T2. T6 & 14.	T2. T8 & 15.
Writing a character sketch	**T1. T11:** To write character sketches, focusing on small details to evoke sympathy or dislike.	**T2. T8:** To write portraits of characters.	T2. T6 & 14.	T2. T8 & 15.

Title of lesson	Y6 objective(s)	Y5 objective(s)/tracking back	Y4	Y3
Using dialogue		**T1. W19:** To explore common vocabulary for introducing and concluding dialogue. **T1. S7:** To develop basic conventions of speech punctuation. **T3. S4:** To use speech marks and other dialogue punctuation appropriately.		
Issues and dilemmas	**T3. T11:** To explore the main issues of a story by writing a story about a dilemma and the issues it raises for the character.			
An introduction to plays	**T1. T13:** To write playscripts, for example using known stories as basis.	**T1. T15:** To write simple playscripts based on own reading and oral work.		T2. T9.
Writing a play	**T1. T13:** To write playscripts, for example using known stories as basis.	**T1. T15:** To write simple playscripts based on own reading and oral work.		T2. T9.
Shape poems		**T1. T14:** To invent calligrams and a range of shape poems, selecting appropriate words and careful presentation.		
Calligrams		**T1. T14:** To invent calligrams and a range of shape poems, selecting appropriate words and careful presentation.		
Rhyming patterns		**T1. T7:** To distinguish between rhyming and non-rhyming poetry and comment on impact of layout.	T1. T7. T2. T9.	T1. T6 & 10. T2. T11.
Water poems	**T1. T14:** To write poems based on personal or imagined experience, linked to poems read.			T3. T9.
Fact and fiction	**T1. T19:** To understand and use the terms 'fact' and 'opinion' and begin to distinguish between the two.	**T1. T17:** To understand the distinction between fact and fiction. To use terms 'fact', 'fiction' and 'non-fiction' appropriately.	T3. T13.	T2. T17.
Non-chronological reports		**T1. T23:** To write simple non-chronological reports from known information.	T3. T21.	T2. T25.
Sequencing instructions		**T2. T14:** To appreciate how written instructions are organised.	T1. T13-15.	T1. T16.
Writing instructions	**T1. T25:** To write clear instructions using conventions learned from reading.	**T2. T16:** To write instructions recognising the importance of correct sequence.	T1. T13, 15, 16 & 18.	T1. T16.
Letter to an author		**T3. T20:** To write letters using appropriate style and vocabulary for the intended reader.		
Writing a formal letter		**T3. T20:** To write letters using appropriate style and vocabulary for the intended reader.		
Explanatory texts	**T2. T25:** To write explanations of a process, using conventions identified through reading.		T2. T21.	
Persuasive writing	**T3. T23:** To present a point of view in writing, linking points persuasively and selecting style and vocabulary appropriate to the reader. **T3. T25:** To design an advertisement.			

Long vowel phonemes

Objectives

Y3. T1-3. W1.
To revise and consolidate the spelling of words containing each of the long vowel phonemes from KS1 (Appendix List 3).

Y3. T2 & 3. W2.
Y4. T2 & 3. W1.
To identify phonemes in speech and writing; blend phonemes for reading and segment words into phonemes for spelling.

Further support
● Put the word cards made before the lesson on to the table so that the children can read them. Where possible, small pictures could be added next to the word, for example: a picture of a bee. Ask the individuals who need extra reinforcement to read the cards. Then ask them to read the cards with the pictures covered.
● Display the lists of long vowel phonemes for reference.
● Use Look-Say-Cover-Write-Check to practise learning the spelling of the words.

Guided work

1. Before the start of the lesson, copy the table of words from the photocopiable sheet opposite to make a set of phoneme word cards.

2. Remind the children about the long vowel phonemes *ee, ea, ai, ie, oa, oo* and *ue* and write these as column headings on the board. Give an example of each: *feet, heat, train, tie, boat, moon, blue*. Then agree with the children in which columns to add the words.

3. Working with the word *feet*, point to the different sounds as you say the word phonetically, *f-ee-t*. Remind the children about the long vowel sound. Repeat this for each of the words. Encourage the children to join in or let them each say a word phonetically to the group.

4. Play a game of charades with the children. Whisper a word from the box on the photocopiable sheet opposite to one of the children. The child then mimes the word to the rest of the group. When the word is guessed, add it to the list (or see if the children can) and whisper a different word to the child who guessed the word correctly to mime to the group.

5. Words in the list with *ee/ea* and *oo/ue* sound the same, for example *boot* and *glue*, so, when adding them to the list, remind the children that these vowel phonemes sound the same but are written differently. Help them to get the correct spelling for the words before adding them to the appropriate list.

Independent work
● Ask the children to write the correct word under each picture on the photocopiable sheet opposite. Encourage the children to say the sentences out loud and work out the words that they need for each sentence phonetically.

Plenary
● Shuffle the word cards and give the children a clue about the word on the top of the pile, for example: *It is something I wear on my foot.* Ask the children to identify the word and try to write it on the board.

Long vowel phonemes

◾ Write the correct words from the box into the sentences.

1. The _____ was buzzing around the _____ .

2. She swept the _____ with the _____ .

3. Sue wore her best _____ when she went to see the _____ .

4. The _____ was reflected in the _____ .

5. The _____ was on the table with the _____ .

6. The old _____ had a new _____ of _____ .

7. The _____ will come out when it _____ .

queen	beach	pie	paint	tail	toast
glue	boat	snail	coat	moon	coat
pool	bee	broom	rains	train	stairs

Word families

Objectives

Y3.T1-3. W1.
To revise and consolidate the spelling of words containing each of the long vowel phonemes from KS1 (Appendix List 3).

Y3. T2 & 3. W2.
Y4. T2 & 3. W1.
To identify phonemes in speech and writing; blend phonemes for reading and segment words into phonemes for spelling.

Guided work

1. Remind the children about the long vowel phonemes *a-e, i-e, o-e* and *u-e*. Give a few examples of each: *cake, skate, bike, kite, pole, globe, tune, cube,* and write these words on the board using the headings: *a-e i-e, o-e, u-e.*

2. Working with the word *cake*, point to the different parts of the word as you sound it out phonetically, c-a-k. Remind the children about the long *a* sound in the word and how it is the 'magic *e*' at the end of the word that tells us how to say the *a* as a long sound. Repeat this for several more *a-e* words, then for other 'magic *e*' words from the board. Encourage the children to join in and say a word phonetically.

3. Ask the children to suggest words to add to each list. Sound out each word phonetically to establish the spelling and decide into which column the word should go. (Some words can be found in the box on the photocopiable sheet opposite.)

4. Remind the children that the 'magic *e*' changes the sound of the vowel in the middle of the word from the short sound to the long sound. As you play with the words to see which are still words without the *e* on the end, such as *bit* and *bite*, *kit* and *kite*, emphasise the different sounds the *i* makes in each word. Say the words so that the children can hear the rhymes, for example: *bite, kite, site, write.*

5. Remember other words have long vowel sounds but are not 'magic *e*' words. You will need to talk to the children about this if any of the words they suggest have spellings using letters other than those in the word families you are covering, for example: *light, fight, bright.*

6. Encourage the children to take turns adding 'magic *e*' words to the appropriate list, for example: *spare, chase, fame, wide, hide.*

Independent work

● Hand out the photocopiable sheet opposite and ask the children to find each thing listed in the box, then write the word next to the object in the picture. Encourage the children to sound the word out phonetically to help them read each word.
● To challenge the children further, ask them to choose five of the words found to write a short sentence about, using the picture to help, for example: *The bike is by the side of the lake.*

Further support
● Display the lists of 'magic *e*' phonemes for reference.

Plenary

● Use the words in the box to find rhyming words to put into families.
● Play with the words to find how many of them are still words when the 'magic *e*' is removed. What sound do they have?

Word families

◼ Can you find the things listed below in the picture? Label the things you find.

cake	lace	fire	phone	skates	bike	hive
rose	gate	knife	dice	mole	lake	mice
pipe	pole	hare	wine	kite	bone	

Happy word families

Objectives

Y3. T1–3. W1.
To revise and consolidate the spelling of words containing each of the vowel phonemes from KS1 (Appendix List 3).

Y3. T2 & 3. W2.
Y4. T2 & 3. W1.
To identify phonemes in speech and writing; blend phonemes for reading and segment words into phonemes for spelling.

Further support

● Underline the vowel phonemes on the cards to make the game easier if necessary. The cards could then be used to play 'Snap'.
● To make the game simpler, put each word family on to a different coloured card.
● Display the lists of vowel phonemes that you did at the beginning of the lesson to help the children remember the word families in the game.
● The game can be played with different groupings and more than once, as there will be a different outcome each time.
● Adapt the game by making cards showing different vowel phonemes.

Guided work

1. Cut the photocopiable sheet opposite into individual cards to make a pack of 36 cards.

2. Remind the children about the vowel phonemes *oo* (as in *good*), *ar*, *oi*, *oy*, *ow* (as in *cow*), *air*, *or*, *er* and *ea* (as in *head*). Give a few examples of each: *wood, stood, bar, far, boil, coil, royal, joy, owl, how, fair, hair, sort, port, her, stern, bread, read*. Write the words on the board under the appropriate headings.

3. Give the children clues about some of the following words which fit into one of the word families on your chart, for example: *This is red liquid that runs through veins in our bodies* (blood). *This person is a funny man you would find in a circus* (clown). *You usually go up these when you go to bed* (stairs). As the children guess each word correctly, ask them to add it to the appropriate list: *spread, jar, blood, star, stairs, perm, toy, fort, tart, flair, soil, head, germ, clown, oil, hood, sport, car, moist, boy, down, dead, stork*. Encourage the children to take turns and, if necessary, help them to sound the words out phonetically to help them spell the words.

Independent work

● Use the cards from the photocopiable sheet opposite to play a game similar to 'Happy families' in groups of three to six. Deal out all the cards. The person to the left of the dealer starts by asking any of the other players for a card containing a specific vowel phoneme – for example, *oi* – to help make a set. The player asking must already have at least one of that word family in their hand. If the player asked has a card from that family, they must hand it over. If that player has two or more cards from that family they only hand over one of them to the other player. The player asking for cards may continue asking any other players until they ask for a card that the other player does not have. The next player to the left then takes their turn to ask for cards. When a player collects all four word family members, the set is placed faced down on the table in front of the player. The player who collects the most word families is the winner!

Plenary

Reinforce the word families at the end of the game.

Happy word families

car	jar	star	tart
cow	owl	towel	clown
head	bread	thread	spread
wood	hood	blood	flood
perm	her	fern	germ
short	stork	fort	port
boil	soil	oil	coil
toy	boy	enjoy	royal
fair	hair	flair	stairs

Double consonant jumble

Objective
Y4. T1. W5.
To spell two-syllable words containing double consonants.

Guided work

1. Enlarge the photocopiable sheet opposite on to card and cut each word into two pieces as indicated. You may need to prepare several sheets if you want the children to work individually or in pairs.

2. Remind the children about 'magic *e*' by looking at words such as: *rob/robe, kit/kite, hid/hide, rid/ride*.

3. Tell them that if we want to keep the vowel sound short we can do this by putting a double consonant after it, for example: *robber, kitten, hidden, riddles*. This stops the magic of 'magic *e*' from changing the vowel sound to a long one.

4. Give the children the pieces of the word jigsaws you prepared earlier and tell them that they need to find the correct ending to each word to make up the jigsaw.

5. Once they have made the words, encourage the children to take turns reading them, sounding them out phonetically to help them read and spell them.

6. Ask them to stick the words on to a sheet of paper and use Look-Say-Cover-Write-Check.

7. Ask the children if they know the meanings of the words and to take turns telling the other children what the words mean. Check if there are words they do not know and explain the meanings as part of your discussion.

Independent work

● For whole-class work or group work, write a simple sentence on the board with one of the double consonant words missing, for example: *The cat was licking her new _____ gently.* Ask the children to suggest the missing word and read out the completed sentence. Individuals could then write the correct word in the space. Then let individuals write a sentence with the double consonant word missing for the rest of the group to suggest the answer.

● For pairs or individual work, ask the children to choose a number of the words (for example, five, eight or ten) and make up simple sentences each with one of the double consonant words in it.

Plenary

Brainstorm some other double consonant words with the children, for example: *galleon, paddle, saddle, hobble, hobby, hassle*. Give the children clues to guess them, for example: *This word begins with the letter 'h' and means to walk with a limp* (hobble).

Further support
● Use the jigsaws regularly to reinforce the reading and spelling of the words. To add variety, use a stopwatch to time how long it takes to make and read the words. Again this can be done with all or just a few of the 24 jigsaws.
● Support the children as they play with the words to make silly sentences for example: *The cat was licking her new kettle gently. The cat was licking her new balloon gently.* Show them how the sentence still makes grammatical sense as the same type of word is being substituted.

Double consonant jumble

bubb	les	ball	oon
gobb	le	comm	on
cobb	ler	mall	et
bobb	in	litt	le
robb	er	holl	ow
wobb	ly	foll	ows
mutt	ers	sudd	en
kett	le	hidd	en
batt	er	midd	le
catt	le	ridd	les
glitt	er	dadd	y
kitt	en	bedd	ing

50 LITERACY HOURS FOR LESS ABLE
LEARNERS: Ages 7-9

Alphabetical order

Guided work

1. Give the children a dictionary each, or one to share with a partner.

2. Ask the children to flick through their dictionaries. Discuss how it is set out. Write the word *apple* on the board and ask the children to find the word in their dictionaries. (Some may need help with this.)

3. Remind the children that words in the dictionary are in alphabetical order. Write the alphabet, in lower-case letters, across the top of the board. Ask the children to look at it and say where in the dictionary they would expect to find the following words (near the beginning, middle or end): *monster, zebra, ant, walk* and *cake*.

4. Explain how the words in dictionaries are arranged when the initial letter is the same, using the second letter in words. Use the words: *snake, sand, still* and *seat* as examples.

5. If it is appropriate, go on to talk about arranging words alphabetically by third then fourth letters.

6. Make a number of word cards using things from around the classroom, for example: *pencil, ruler, chair, desk, rubber, crayon, book* and *paper*. Allocate a word card to each child and ask them to hold it up on their chest and get themselves into alphabetical order.

Independent work

● For pairs or individual work, give the children one of the activities opposite, along with the alphabet, and ask them to cut out and arrange the words in alphabetical order before sticking them on to paper. Choose the exercise most appropriate to the individual's ability. If appropriate, this activity could be adapted for use on computer.

Plenary

● Play 'Dictionary challenge' by giving the children a simple dictionary each. Choose the name of one of the children in the group, for example: Sarah. Write it clearly on the board and then ask the children to find where Sarah would fit in the dictionary. The child who finds the correct place first then chooses another name from the group for them all to find where it would fit.

● Discuss other contexts where alphabetical order is used, for example: the class register, address books, phone directories.

Alphabetical order

a b c d e f g h i j k l m n o p q r s t u v w x y z

Activity A
First and second letters:

sun	bat	big	cut
bun	cat	pig	cot
fun	sat	fig	put

Activity B
First, second and third letters:

lamb	ball	cry	clap	leak
bat	lake	bean	crab	meat
man	mat	bell	dawn	cat

Activity C
First, second, third and fourth letters:

Rogers	Appley	Roberts	Stern
Salt	Regis	Salmon	Abbey
Abbott	Reed	Stevens	Appleton

Capital letters and full stops

Objectives
Y3. T1. S11.
To write in complete sentences.

Y3. T1. S12.
To demarcate the end of a sentence with a full stop and the start of a new one with a capital letter.

Guided work

1. Make the children two simple cards each. On the first write: *CAPITAL LETTERS* and on the second draw a large dot (a full stop). Copy this short paragraph on to the board (leaving out the full stops and capital letters):

> the butcher was running down the road he was chasing after a little dog he had a piece of meat in his mouth

2. Ask the children to read the words *CAPITAL LETTERS* on their first card. Tell them that you have written it all in capital letters to remind them what the lesson is about. Ask if they remember when we use capital letters in writing. Focus upon the use of capital letters at the beginning of sentences.

3. Invite the children to look at the second card. Ask if they know what it is. If they are unsure, remind them that it is something that we think about along with capital letters when we are writing sentences: we use full stops at the end of sentences.

4. Show the children the paragraph on the board. Read it to them as it is written, with no punctuation. Ask if this sounds right. Discuss why it sounds wrong, then read it slowly, pausing where sentences finish. Discuss if this sounds better and why.

5. Tell the children you are going to read the paragraph again slowly and, as you do this, you want them to hold up the capital-letters or the full-stop card where they think you need to correct the text.

6. Encourage the children to hold up their capital-letters card with the first word (*the*) and continue to read slowly through the text.

7. Tell the children that, as you read the text again, you are going to add the capital letters and full stops in a different colour when they hold up the cards. Discuss the end result.

Independent work

● Give the children one of the exercises on the photocopiable sheet opposite according to their ability. Ask them to read the paragraph and then add the capital letters and full stops. Ask the children to leave the two cards on the table to remind them.

Plenary

● Read slowly through the paragraphs on the photocopiable sheet opposite for the children to hold up their capital-letters and full-stop cards in the appropriate places.

Further support
● Use the exercises as graded lessons to reinforce and progress the learning process.

Capital letters and full stops

Activity A
■ Add the capital letters and full stops to this paragraph.

the children went for a walk to the park as soon as they got there one of the boys

fell he twisted his ankle very badly two of the children stayed to look after him the

others quickly ran to fetch help

Activity B
■ Add the capital letters and full stops to this paragraph.

the children crept out of the small door they found themselves in a beautiful forest

they both stopped and stared at the amazing sight they had just left an ordinary

little house now they were standing in an overgrown jungle sarah was lost for words

but freddy yelled out in surprise

Activity C
■ Add the capital letters and full stops to this paragraph.

gemma had decided that she didn't want to go to the party her two friends wanted

to know why at first she wouldn't answer she just hid her face in her hands then she

whispered that she didn't want to go because she had nothing to wear the others

just looked at each other and started to laugh gemma got very cross she wanted to

know what was so funny sal then said that a shopping trip had been arranged for

that afternoon they were all going to buy something new to wear a big grin

appeared on gemma's face

More capitalisation

Objective
Y3. T2. S8.
To use capitalisation from reading, for example, names, headings, special emphasis.

Guided work

1. Copy these words and phrases in large, lower-case print on the board: *get out!*, *mr bennet, i know, jasper morris, the daily planet, oh! the grand old duke of york.*

2. Make cards with the capital letters *G, E, T, O, U, T, M, B, I, J, M, T, D, P, O, T, G, O, D, Y* on them.

3. Ask the children to look at the words on the board and see if they think the words are written correctly.

4. Revise when we use capital letters: at the beginning of a sentence, for the first person 'I', names, days of the week, months of the year, festivals, headings, titles of books and films, for special emphasis. Discuss each one and give contextual examples, perhaps including the use of labels and names on displays around the room, books showing their titles, newspaper headings and so on, to help the children understand the different places that we use capital letters.

5. Show the children the letter cards and tell them that they are going to help you find which words they fit. Then individuals can stick them over the appropriate small-case letter.

6. Work through the words explaining, or asking the children to explain, why a capital letter is needed. Tell them that *GET OUT!* is written all in capital letters to emphasise the command. (Explain that capital letters can be used in writing to show words that are being shouted, for example.)

Independent work

● Give the children one of the photocopiable activities opposite according to their ability. Ask them to read the text carefully and then to add all the capital letters in an easily visible colour.

Plenary

● Give the children an assortment of capital-letter cards and, as you say individual names of children in the class, ask any child with that capital letter to hold it up, for example: Who has the capital letter card that starts the name Sarah?
● Go through one, or both, of the exercises orally or give the children the answers to self-correct.

Further support
● For whole-class work or group work, use one of the activities copied on to acetate to discuss the use of capital letters.
● Use the exercises as graded lessons for reinforcement and progression.
● Make a wall chart to explain when we use capital letters.
● Ask the children to write their own name, pet's name or best friend's name. Encourage them to write their own labels for their drawers or coat-pegs and so on.

More capitalisation

Activity A
◀ Add the capital letters to these sentences.

1. my best friend is called preya.
2. i went to alton towers yesterday.
3. my birthday is in march.
4. my favourite film is lord of the rings.
5. dad asked wayne to come with us.
6. natalie and i are going to the match on saturday.
7. i went to the shop in new street to buy the new magazine called 'all yours'.
8. after falling, mrs jones was shouting 'help!' for ages before anyone heard her.
9. the headline in the newspaper read 'beckham to manage england – exclusive!'
10. greg and i went to see the film 'honey, i lost the goldfish' last saturday.
11. everyone agreed that mr smart was the best teacher at calton junior school.
12. 'he's behind you!' bellowed the audience at the pantomime, mother goose.
13. 'terry injured!' was plastered all over the newspapers.
14. the teacher told the class to sing 'twinkle, twinkle little star'.

Activity B
◀ Add the capital letters to this paragraph.

on match day the tension began to build as the excited fans jostled towards the stadium. it had finally come! the day of the biggest match of the season, between barkford united and pentland hotshoes. adam, robbie and mr james, their dad, had got the tickets from mr webb, their football coach. as they went through the turnstile they could hear the crowd beginning to chant "barkford boys are the best, yes the best!" adam and robbie joined in. then at the end of the song they yelled "united for the cup!" so loud that mr james had to cover his ears.

Remember verbs?

Objectives

Y3. T1. S3.
To explore the function of verbs in sentences.

Y3. T1. S5.
To use the term 'verb' appropriately.

Y4. T1. S2.
To investigate verb tenses: (past, present and future).

Guided work

1. Ask the children if they can remember what a verb is. Share some simple examples: *run, sleep, stand* and so on.

2. Remind the children of these points.

- Verbs are either action words or tell us about a condition or state, for example: we jog, they slept, she is frightened, I will go. Verbs have a tense to tell us when the action takes place.
- The *past tense* tells us what has already happened. This might be five minutes ago, yesterday, last week or years ago, for example: I jumped, she slipped, they drove.
- The *present tense* tells us what is happening now: I am walking, he is smiling. Or: I walk, he smiles.
- The *future tense* tells us what will happen (tomorrow, next week), for example: I will go for a walk, I will visit my gran.

3. Play a game of 'Simon says' using a range of physical actions, for example: *march on the spot, wink, wave your arms in the air, put your hand on your head, wiggle your bottom, put your finger in your ear, bend your knees, wiggle your fingers* and *turn around*.

4. After playing the game look at some of these verbs. Make them into sentences, verbally, to show what they are like in the past tense and then the present tense, for example: *Yesterday, I walked to my friend's house. I walk in time to the music.*

Independent work

- Work through the first picture on the photocopiable sheet opposite together, reading the sentences to see which fits the picture. Then ask the children to work through the rest of the pictures and matching pairs of sentences. Ask them to draw lines in one colour for past tense and another for present.
- To challenge more confident children, give them only the pictures from the sheet and ask them to write their own past and present sentences. Encourage them to use words such as now and yesterday.

Plenary

- Go through the activity orally and underline the verbs on an enlarged or acetate copy of the photocopiable sheet opposite. Identify and read the pairs, for example: is walking, walked.
- Play 'Simon says' again.
- Work to put some of the verbs into the future tense.

Further support

- Display a list of some common verbs the children may be familiar with under the headings 'past tense' and 'present tense'.
- Ask the children to cut out the sentence strips and paste them in pairs, so they can compare the spellings of verbs in different tenses.

Remember verbs?

◼ Draw coloured lines to match the sentences to the pictures. Use a different colour for past and present tenses.

The woman is **washing** her car.

The dog **jumped** over the wall.

The baby **played** with his rattle.

The cat **chased** the mouse.

The man **walked** up the hill.

The cat is **chasing** the mouse.

The woman **washed** her car.

The girl **kicks** the ball.

The dog is **jumping** over the wall.

The man is **walking** up a hill.

The baby is **playing** with his rattle.

The girl **kicked** the ball.

50 LITERACY HOURS FOR LESS ABLE
LEARNERS: Ages 7-9

Past, present and future

Objectives
Y3. T1. S4.
To use verb tenses with increasing accuracy in speaking and writing.

Y3. T1. S5.
To use the term 'verb' appropriately.

Guided work

1. Remind the children that verbs are action words or words that tell us about the condition or state of someone or something, for example: *they sleep, she is frightened, I was cold.*

2. Remind them that verbs have tense to tell us whether the action was done yesterday, last week or years ago (in the past), or whether the action is being done now (in the present).

3. Recap on the rules for creating past and present tenses of verbs and any spelling issues (for example, double consonants). Try to cover both regular and the main irregular verbs, for example: *to be, to go.*

4. Next, tell the children how the future tense is formed, focusing on using *will* and *am going to.* Remember to spend time on the more common irregular verbs.

5. Work with three children from the group. Ask the first child to give you a sentence in the present tense, encouraging the child to use imagination to make a game out of it, for example: *I am an astronaut* or, *I play for Manchester United.* Challenge the second child to put the first sentence into the past tense and the third child to put it into the future tense.

6. Revisit and scribe the sentences for the children. Underline the verbs and spend some time discussing the differences between the tenses and how they are formed and spelled. (You might find that the construction *I am going to* comes up. If so, spend time discussing the difference between *I am going to* and *I am going to go to.*)

7. Repeat the activity with the children swapping roles, but this time ask them also to say whether their statements are in the past, present or future tense. Once the activity is flowing well, work on second and third person sentences by challenging the children to turn each other's sentences into second or third person.

Independent work

● Ask the children to underline the appropriate verb tense in each sentence on the photocopiable sheet opposite. Encourage the children to say the sentences out loud to check their answers.

● To challenge the children further, ask them to write past, present or future at the end of the sentence after deciding which tense of the verb to use.

Plenary

Go through the exercise orally in a group or class situation or have another round of the game you played during the lesson.

Further support
● Display a chart of familiar verbs (including the ones in the activity) in their past, present and future forms to discuss as you work with the group.
● Ask the children to use Look-Say-Cover-Write-Check to practise the verb tenses on the sheet.

Past, present and future

◀ Underline the correct verb tense in each of the following sentences.

1. The boy **walked, is walking, will walk** to the park yesterday.

2. Tomorrow Pat **watched, is watching, will watch** her favourite pop star on TV.

3. The bus **stopped, is stopping, will stop** at the bus stop and then went on to London.

4. The snowman **looked, looks, will look** good now he is finished.

5. The baby **played, is playing, will play** with her ball after she has had her sleep.

6. The boy **hugged, is hugging, will hug** his new puppy as soon as he gets him.

7. This morning Winston **jumped, is jumping, will jump** in a high jump competition and won.

8. Last year children all over the world **ordered, are ordering, will order** millions of burgers.

9. The writer **typed, is typing, will type** his story at this very moment.

10. Probably Sandra **cried, is crying, will cry** if she falls off her bike.

11. It **rained, is raining, will rain** so I will not go out just yet.

12. The twig **tapped, is tapping, will tap** on the window last night when it was windy.

13. Earlier today Colin **cleaned, is cleaning, will clean** his car.

14. The boy **laughed, is laughing, will laugh** at the clown he is watching.

15. They **whispered, are whispering, will whisper** all night and kept me awake.

50 LITERACY HOURS FOR LESS ABLE LEARNERS: Ages 7-9

Irregular verbs

Objective
Y4. T1. W8.
To spell irregular tense changes.

Guided work

1. Remind the children about the function of the verb and give some examples: *Sally loved her kitten, Ali walks to school every day, Harry will travel to Spain for his holiday.*

2. Remind them that many verb forms follow a pattern when we use them in the past, present and future tenses. Write these up on the board and discuss the pattern:

Verb	Past	Present	Future
To walk	walked	is walking/walks	will walk
To frown	frowned	is frowning/frowns	will frown
To peer	peered	is peering/peers	will peer
To shudder	shuddered	is shuddering/shudders	will shudder
To jump	jumped	is jumping/jumps	will jump

3. Tell the children that there are also many verbs that do not follow this regular pattern and that these are called irregular verbs. They do not follow the usual pattern when we use them in the past, present and future tenses and we have to learn how these verbs change.

4. Display a chart of these irregular verbs and discuss how they do not fit into the regular pattern like the ones above. Remind the children that the verbs must agree with the nouns or pronouns, for example: *I am going, she went, they will meet.*

Verb	Past	Present	Future
To go	went	go/goes	will go
To be	was/were	am/is/are	will be
To come	came	am/is/are coming/come/comes	will come
To speak	spoke	am/is/are speaking/speak/speaks	will speak
To meet	met	meet/meets	will meet
To do	did	am/is/are doing do/does	will do

5. Point out to the children that we use these all the time, without thinking about it, in our everyday speech.

Independent work

● After discussing irregular verbs, work through the three examples at the top of the photocopiable sheet opposite orally with the group. Then ask them to underline the appropriate verb tense in each sentence in the exercise that follows.

Plenary

Ask the children to sit in a circle. Choose a volunteer to begin by saying a short sentence, for example: *I went for a walk.* The person on the left then has to say the sentence in the past tense, and the person on the left again has to say it in the future tense. The next person starts again with another sentence in the present tense.

Further support
● As the children meet other irregular verbs add them to the display.
● Give the children as much opportunity to verbalise the irregular verbs as possible, and use them in the first, second and third person to get them used to the different forms.

Irregular verbs

- Next week I **spoke, speak, will speak** to my friend in Australia.
- Because she was ill she **was not able, is not able, will not be able** to go to the party yesterday.
- They **swam, are swimming, will swim** in the race as we speak.

■ Underline the correct verb tense in each of the following sentences.

1. The gang **went, go, will go** to the match next Saturday.

2. Last Friday Jason **came, comes, will come** home shattered after his judo class.

3. The police officer is **drove, driving, will drive** at the speed limit.

4. Last night Greg **was, is, will be** glad to be home after a horrid day at school.

5. Kate **met, meets, will meet** Kim as they were on their way to the cinema.

6. Jim is beginning to get nervous as he **spoke, speaks, will speak** to the whole school later this morning.

7. I **came, comes, will come** if I can.

8. The crowd watches as the ship **sunk, sinks, will sink** without trace.

9. Simon **wrote, writes, will write** to thank his gran for the present first thing tomorrow morning.

10. Kye peered into the darkness as he **opened, is opening, will open** the attic door.

11. Tim and Raj were **doing, are doing, will do** their homework now so that they can go and play football later.

12. Katrina **woke, is waking, will wake** up as she had a strange dream.

13. They **slept, sleep, will sleep** in the attic when they visit next week.

14. John **said, says, will say** he was happy to help.

15. They **met, meet, will meet** in the park every Saturday.

50 LITERACY HOURS FOR LESS ABLE LEARNERS: Ages 7-9

Powerful verbs

Guided work

1. Remind the children that verbs are usually the most important part of a sentence. They tell us what characters are doing, how they feel, and about the condition or state they are in, for example: *The boy jumped over the gate. The girl smiled at her friend. The baby laughed when he was tickled.*

2. Tell the children that when we are writing any piece of work, whether it is a story, a newspaper article or a letter, we can make it more exciting and give the reader a better picture of what is happening by using powerful verbs rather than simple ones, for example: *hobbled* instead of *went, exclaimed* instead of *said, scorched* instead of *burnt.*

3. Write the three short example sentences above on the board. Discuss different ideas of changing the verbs in these sentences with the children or model the following examples. Change the verb *jumped* in the sentence, *'The boy jumped over the gate'*, to *hurdled* and the readers will have a much more vivid picture in their minds of how the boy got over the gate. Similarly, in the second example, *beamed* could be used instead of *smiled,* and, in the third sentence, *giggled* could be used instead of *laughed.*

Independent work

● Ask the children to identify and underline the verb in each sentence on the photocopiable sheet, then choose the most appropriate powerful verb from the box at the top of the page and write the new verb above the original one.

Plenary

● Make a chart with the children to show the different powerful verbs which could be used instead of a particular verb, for example: if you choose *walk* you could get the children to suggest alternatives such as: *hobble, trudge, amble, hike, march, hoof it, promenade, saunter, stride, stroll, traipse, tramp, trek.* Use the opportunity to introduce the children to a simple thesaurus and show them that this will help them to choose more powerful verbs.

Powerful verbs

◼ Use these powerful verbs to make the sentences more interesting.

> sobbed   pounced   marched   flung   crept   exploded
>
> dozed   steered   hobbled   grinned   was ripped   fled

1. My dog slept on the sofa.	**7.** An old woman walked down the road.
2. The girl smiled at her new dress.	**8.** The bomb burst with a big boom.
3. A man walked quickly down the lane.	**9.** The cat jumped on the mouse.
4. The boy threw his frisbee across the sky.	**10.** This book was torn in half.
5. The baby cried loudly.	**11.** The thief left the country.
6. The children walked into the cave.	**12.** The man drove his car into the garage.

50 LITERACY HOURS FOR LESS ABLE
LEARNERS: Ages 7–9

Question or exclamation?

Objectives

Y3. T1. S6.
To secure knowledge of question marks and exclamation marks in reading, understand their purpose and use appropriately in own writing.

Y4. T3. S3.
To understand how the grammar of a sentence alters when the sentence type is altered, when, for example a statement is made into a question.

Guided work

1. Write a few questions on the board, for example: *What is your name? Where do you live? Who is your best friend?* Ask the children how they would respond.

2. Ask the children if they remember looking at questions and question marks before. Remind them that a question mark replaces a full stop and that a question is a sentence which needs another sentence – the answer.

3. Remind the children of the sort of words which begin questions, for example: *who, what, where, when, how, are you, shall we, will they* and so on. Play a riddle game. Say to the children: *This is the answer to a question, so what could the question be?* Then give them an answer, for example: *I have a pet cat.* Think of a few more answers for them to form questions from, for example: *I have blue eyes. Sometimes I like to swim.* This will help the children to recognise how to construct questions.

4. Now write a few exclamations on the board, for example: *Don't do that! Hold that door open! Help! Come on England!*

5. Ask if they remember looking at exclamations and exclamation marks before. Remind them that an exclamation mark is used instead of a full stop for emphasis, to draw attention to the words and show us how they should be read or said.

6. Ask the children to stand up and shape themselves into a question mark and then an exclamation mark. Ask them to make the correct shape as you read out short questions or exclamations one at a time, or write them on the board, for example: *Don't jump, Grab this rope, Where is my scarf, Will you stop that, Who is at the door, How did you do that, Keep out, We won.*

Further support

● Make a chart to show a range of different questions. Underline the words which start the questions as well as the question marks at the end, as these will give the children a clue about whether the sentences are questions or not.
● Make a chart of exclamations.

Independent work

● Give the children one of the exercises on the photocopiable sheet and ask them to use a different coloured pen to add question marks or exclamation marks to each sentence.

Plenary

● Ask the children to take turns to give an answer for the rest of the group to think of the question, as you did in the main activity.
● Alternatively, give each child a card with a question mark on it and one with an exclamation mark. As you say a simple sentence or question, ask the children to hold up the card that is appropriate, for example: *What is her name? This is great!*

Question or exclamation?

Activity A

■ Using different coloured pens, add question marks or exclamation marks to these sentences.

1. Who are you

2. You should have seen the parade

3. United won 16:0

4. Is that Mel over there

5. How much change did you get

6. Jess, you look great in that dress

7. Did Sam miss the bus

8. Does this train go to London

9. Stop that man

10. Hold tight please

11. I just don't believe it

12. Will you hold my coat, please

13. Where did you buy that hat

14. Wait for me

Activity B

■ Using different coloured pens, add question and exclamation marks to this paragraph.

I knew no one would believe me, but I really am telling the truth___ I did see a spaceship___ How did I know it was something from outer space___ I know it was because it was like nothing on this planet. The lights were more dazzling than you could imagine. Wow___ I never knew lights could be so bright. Then what do you think happened___ As it hovered above the ground, small creatures started to float down towards me. What was I to do___ Well, there was only one thing to do – run, of course, as fast as I could___ But they followed me___ I sensed something breathing down my neck and I didn't know what to do. Should I turn round and look or just run as fast as I could___ What would you have done___ I decided to look around and what do you think I saw___ It was so amazing I can hardly describe it___

Speech bubbles

Objective
Y3. T1. S9.
To notice and investigate other devices for presenting texts, for example speech bubbles.

Guided work

1. Before the lesson draw and cut out about six large speech bubbles (big enough to write a line of speech on and hold up as though a child is speaking). If possible, collect a few cartoon strips from newspapers, comics, or story books presented in the form of cartoons.

2. Show the children one of the shapes you have cut out. Ask them what they think it is. If they do not recognise it, tell them that it is a speech bubble and it is one way of showing what someone is saying.

3. Share the cartoon strips collected. Ask the children if they know why some sentences are written in the bubbles. If they do not know, tell them that they are the words that the characters actually say. Tell them that the story is told mainly through the characters talking to each other.

4. With suggestions from the children, plan a meeting between two or three people. Think about what each would say. Then with a large marker pen write the exact words spoken on to the different bubbles, for example:

> Hi Freddy, shall we go to the park?
> Oh, hi Ravi, I'd love to, but I have to go to the shop.
> What if I come with you and then we'll go to the park?
> Yeah! That'd be cool.
> Shall we call for Kim after we've taken your shopping home?
> Great idea! Let's get going!

5. Ask for volunteers, two or three at a time, to come out and hold the bubbles to their mouths as the rest of the group read the speech bubbles. Tell them that the words people say to each other in conversation are called dialogue.

Independent work

● In pairs, give the children enlarged copies of the photocopiable sheet and ask them to rehearse what the characters in the pictures might be saying to each other. Then ask them to write the dialogue they have agreed on.

Plenary

● Go through the activity orally, in a group or class situation, to show that the characters can all use different dialogue and still be correct.
● Write a class or group cartoon strip of a knock-knock joke, or a scene from a class book or a soap opera, to be displayed in the classroom.

Further support
● Let the children look at more comic strips to reinforce understanding of speech.
● Integrate little characters with speech bubbles into your classroom displays. They could be reminding the children about different language skills you have covered.
● Before starting the photocopiable sheet opposite, get the children to tell the story from looking at the pictures. Alternatively, read them a simple version of the tale. Then introduce the idea of what the characters may actually say to each other.

Speech bubbles

What do you think these fairy-tale characters are saying?

50 LITERACY HOURS FOR LESS ABLE
LEARNERS: Ages 7-9

Speech marks

Objectives
Y3. T1. S7.
To secure the knowledge of basic conventions of speech punctuation.

Y3. T1. S8.
To use the term 'speech marks'.

Guided work

1. Recap the work on speech bubbles and dialogue (see page 32), then share the story extract on the photocopiable sheet on page 118, focusing on the dialogue. Perhaps ask volunteers to read out the dialogue as you re-read the text.

2. Write these sentences on the board, omitting the speech marks:

- 'Walk, don't run, in that corridor,' shouted the teacher.
- The policeman yelled, 'Stop, in the name of the Law!'
- 'Where am I?' asked the boy. 'I think I'm lost.'
- Manisha squealed, 'Don't ever sneak up on me like that again.'
- 'Did I imagine it,' said Greg, 'or did your mum say yes?'

3. What do the children notice about the sentences? Remind them of the dialogue in the photocopiable sheet on page 118. If they do not realise that they all contain speech, tell the children and read the sentences again with more intonation.

4. Ask the children if they remember what punctuation we use to show that someone is speaking. Point out the speech marks in the text on photocopiable page 118, for example.

5. Go through the sentences on the board slowly, asking where speech marks should go. As you do this, identify the other punctuation in each sentence. Use a different coloured pen to add the speech marks so they can be seen clearly. Demonstrate that speech marks go around the actual words that are spoken, opening and closing the speech in the same way that they are isolated in speech bubbles.

6. Re-read the sentences and ask the children to indicate where the speech marks go using their fingers in the air (as we do when we quote).

Independent work

- Give the children one of the activities from the photocopiable sheet and ask them to use a coloured pen to put speech marks in the appropriate places.
- To challenge the children further, ask them to continue the dialogue in Activity B.

Plenary

- Use Post-it Notes to cover the punctuation in a section of dialogue in a Big Book or on photocopiable page 118 and reveal it as the children work out what punctuation marks are appropriate.

Further support
- This may be a difficult concept for some children to grasp. They will need much reinforcement of the work, using other examples, before they begin to fully understand the purpose of speech marks and are able to use them themselves.
- Show the children simple dialogue, where it appears in stories, to help them understand all the punctuation used with speech marks and to pinpoint where the punctuation is placed.

Speech marks

Activity A
◼ Use a coloured pen to add speech marks to these sentences.

1. Please wait by the gate, ordered the teacher.

2. Tim shouted, wait for me!

3. Don't give it me, Jade exclaimed. I know I'll drop it.

4. I hope you can read my map, said Ali.

5. Holly whispered, I'm sure that noise is getting nearer.

6. Do you want a sweet? asked Dean. They are gorgeous.

7. The toddler sobbed, I've lost my mummy!

8. Jump in the car, Dad yelled, or you won't get there on time.

Activity B
◼ Use a coloured pen to add speech marks to this paragraph.

As the children were walking in the park, Jake suddenly stopped. I've forgotten the

crisps! he gasped.

Don't worry, soothed Ali. I've brought plenty of sandwiches.

Yes, and I've got lots of sausage rolls, Sal added.

Grinning from ear to ear, Raj chuckled, Well, with all that plus the cola and biscuits

I've got, I don't think we'll miss the crisps. Do you?

No! they all replied together.

Commas in lists

Objectives
Y3. T1. S13.
To use commas to separate
items in a list.

Guided work

1. Write the following sentences (leaving out the commas) on the board. You could use a magnetic board or interactive whiteboard:

- There was a puppy a kitten some fish a few hamsters and a rabbit in the pet shop.
- She bought a sweater a pair of trousers a pair of shoes and a new coat.
- In the toyshop window there was a doll's house a train set a board game and a teddy bear.
- The books on the shelf were *The EGC The Fools Simon and the Sweet Factory* and *Harry and the Huge Strawberry*.

2. Ask the children to look at the sentences as you read them. Ask if they notice anything - the lists. Discuss which items make up each list and underline them. If working interactively, they could be pulled out of the sentence and put in a vertical list, then put back in.

3. Ask the children if they remember what punctuation marks we use to separate items in a list. Demonstrate how commas help us to read by breaking up the sentence.

4. Tell the children that we use a comma after each item in a list until we get to the word *and*, which we put instead of a comma; this is just before the last item in the list. Remind the children that items may be more than just a word (for example, *tablecloth*); it may be a phrase (for example, *a bag of frozen peas*).

5. Work through the sentences with the children, putting the commas in the appropriate places using a coloured pen.

6. Give each child a piece of card and ask them to draw a large comma on it. Read the sentences slowly with the children and ask them to indicate where the commas go by holding up their cards as you read.

Further support
● Use some items around the classroom, such as a pencil, a pen, a rubber, a sharpener, and make some small cards with commas and the word *and* written on them. Let the children make visual 'sentences' with the objects and comma cards.

Independent work

● Give the children Activity A and ask them to use a coloured pen to put the commas in the appropriate places.
● To challenge the children further ask them to complete the sentences in the second activity with their own lists. Perhaps they coul discuss the various categories in pairs or small groups first.

Plenary

● Ask the children to hold up their comma cards as you read out the sentences in the first activity opposite together.

Commas in lists

Activity A

■ Use a coloured pen to add commas to these lists.

1. The children were told to take their swimsuit towel and hairbrushes to the pool.

2. I invited Sam Jane Sophie and Ben to come to my birthday party.

3. The teacher dropped his pen book pencil ruler and rubber.

4. The garden was full of flowers like roses pansies primroses and daisies.

5. The trees in the wood were mainly oak beech silver birch maple and ash.

6. We saw lions tigers pumas cheetahs and leopards in the wildlife park.

7. In the dining room there were six chairs a table a dresser a fireplace and a lamp.

8. The small boy had a sore throat a very bad headache a rash across his face a terrible cough and a runny nose, so his mother sent for the doctor.

Activity B

■ Finish off these sentences with a list of things.

1. My favourite clothes are _____

_____

2. For my breakfast I like to have _____

_____

3. My favourite films are _____

_____

4. People and pets living in my house are _____

_____

5. My best friends are _____

_____

Other comma uses

Objectives

Y3. T2. S7.
To use the term 'comma' appropriately in relation to reading.

Y3. T3. S7.
To become aware of the use of commas in marking grammatical boundaries within sentences.

Y4. T1. S5.
To practise using commas to mark grammatical boundaries within sentences.

Guided work

1. Draw a large comma on the board and ask the children what it is. Remind them how commas are used in lists. Explain that commas are also used to separate phrases so that the meaning is clear. Commas indicate a pause when reading.

2. Write the following sentences on the board:

- The children went on the sailing boat the *Maid Marion*.
- The policeman PC Plod collected his award for bravery.

3. Ask the children to look at the sentences as you read them (pausing slightly where the commas would go). Discuss that the *Maid Marion* is the same as *the sailing boat* and *PC Plod* is the *policeman*. Read out the sentences again missing out one then the other. Discuss the fact that the sentences still make sense. Explain that they are just adding more detail and so we put commas around them.

4. Discuss where the commas should be and add them in a colour:

- The children went on the sailing boat, the *Maid Marion*.
- The policeman, PC Plod, collected his award for bravery.

5. Then work through the following sentences in the same way:

- The girl who had been out in the rain stamped her wet feet.
- That dog the one with the shaggy coat ran down the street.

6. Explain that the commas mark phrases in the sentences that add more detail and that these could be left out. Discuss the phrases which could be omitted and read the sentences without them.

- The girl, who had been out in the rain, stamped her wet feet.
- That dog, the one with the shaggy coat, ran down the street.

Independent work

- Ask the children to put the commas in the appropriate places in the first activity on the photocopiable sheet.
- To challenge the children further, ask them to cut out and make the complex sentences in the second activity, inserting the commas.

Plenary

- Read out the sentences in the first activity opposite and ask the children to indicate where the commas go by holding up their cards.

Further support
- Remind the children to try reading the sentences and omitting the part that could fit in commas.
- This concept is difficult for many children to grasp and may lead to the 'pepper pot of commas' syndrome! It will probably need further teaching and reinforcement work.
- Use a poster of an explanation and examples for the children's reference.

Other comma uses

Activity A
■ Use a coloured pen to add commas to these sentences.

1. The room the one on the left by the front door was icily cold.

2. The Lord Mayor Bill Simpson was opening the school fair.

3. I went to see Mrs Janes my old infant teacher.

4. It was very strange as the table which was full of food was also thick with dust.

5. The flowers roses and carnations were pretty shades of pink.

6. We all thought it was terrible that Matt Slater United's manager had been sacked.

7. The dress which was blue and white was right in the middle of the shop window.

8. The TV presenter making a comeback after his car accident was very nervous.

9. Kevin usually so accurate when kicking a ball misjudged it and broke the window.

10. Even the fire brigade normally so calm and efficient seemed to be rushing everywhere in panic.

Activity B
■ Combine these muddled beginnings, middles and ends into complete sentences and add the commas where appropriate:

I haven't seen you in ages!	Simon	Well	My sister
is now in hospital.	Jacky	The boy	is older than me

What is an adjective?

Objectives
Y3. T2. S2.
To identify and explore the function of adjectives within sentences.

Y3. T2. S3.
To use the term 'adjective' appropriately.

Guided work

1. Write a list of nouns on one side of the board, for example: *man, baby, book, chair, garden, toy, potato, children, room.* List a selection of adjectives on the other side, for example: *young, tired, crying, creaking, wooden, tiny, happy, untidy, beautiful, ugly, huge.*

2. Point to the list of nouns as you read them. Ask the children if they remember what sort of words these are (nouns).

3. Point to the list of adjectives as you read them. Explain that these are adjectives and that they tell us more about nouns.

4. Play with the list of nouns and adjectives making sensible phrases, and then 'nonsense' phrases. An interactive whiteboard would allow for fun experimentation here, for example: *a wooden chair, an untidy garden, a beautiful baby, a happy chair, a crying book, a creaking potato.* Point out how the adjectives are telling us more about the nouns. Use other nouns and adjectives that the children suggest. Also point to or hold up items from the classroom so that the children have a visual reference and ask them to say (describe) what they are, for example: *a plastic chair, an orange crayon, a good boy.*

Further support
● Remind the children to read through the sentences, trying different adjectives until they find the most appropriate one.
● To support this work, you could use the photocopiable sheets from the back of the book, such as 108, 110 and 111. Notice some of the adjectives used in the extracts and ask the children to substitute alternative ones, perhaps for comic effect.
● Put up a poster to remind the children that adjectives tell us about nouns.

Independent work
● Ask the children to underline the noun in each sentence on the photocopiable sheet opposite and write the appropriate adjective in the space, or they could cut out the adjectives that are in the box and stick them into the appropriate spaces.

Plenary
● Go through the activity orally, in a group or class situation.
● Experiment with a few of the sentences from the photocopiable sheet asking the children to choose the 'correct' and then 'nonsense' adjectives, noticing that the sentence still makes grammatical sense because they are replacing the same type of word in terms of its function within the sentence.

What is an adjective?

◼ Underline the noun(s) in each sentence. Then add the most appropriate adjective(s) from the box.

> rickety   flickering   excited   vivid
>
> old   lame   purring   front
>
> beautiful   deserted   blue   loud   kind

1. The _____ boys went to the football match.

2. I'm painting my _____ door.

3. She wore a _____ dress.

4. We saw a _____ dog limping down the road.

5. The _____ table wobbled when anyone went near it.

6. A train stopped in the _____ station.

7. The _____ boy helped the _____ woman across the road.

8. The _____ candle sent smoke high up into the air.

9. Can you see how this artist liked to use _____ colours?

10. There was _____ music playing at the disco.

11. The _____ cat sat on his owner's lap.

12. A _____ scent from the flowers filled the air.

Powerful adjectives

Objectives
Y3. T2. T2.
To refer to significant aspects of the text, for example opening, build-up, atmosphere, and to know language is used to create these, for example use of adjectives for description.

Y4. T2. S1.
To revise and extend work on adjectives from Year 3, Term 2 and work on expressive and figurative language.

Guided work

1. Remind the children about the work covered in 'What is an adjective?' on page 40. Look again at the list of adjectives you made.

2. Concentrate on just one of the adjectives (for example, *tired*). Ask for suggestions of other words that mean the same or similar. Encourage the children to use a thesaurus, showing them how to use it and listing some of the alternative words and phrases. If they find this too difficult, give them some words (for example: *shattered, exhausted, done in, jaded, weary, spent, worn out, dead on my feet*).

3. Discuss why synonyms are useful (for better precision or accuracy, for the sound of the word, because a different word may be more powerful, or a different word is needed because the obvious one has already been used). Choose some figurative or expressive phrases.

4. Pick out and discuss the effect of some of the powerful adjectives used in the story extracts on photocopiable pages 115, 117 and 118.

5. Write a few more figurative and expressive words and phrases on the board (for example: *ecstatic, as pleased as Punch, as pretty as a picture* and so on). If appropriate, ask the children to show in their facial or body expressions what the adjective describes (for example, *thrilled to bits*). Tell the children that words and phrases like these are expressive because we use strong, vivid language. Figurative language is the use of a metaphor or simile to create an image.

6. Write these sentences on the board. Discuss the differences with the children and ask which sentences are better and why:

- The leaf had turned from green to brown.
- The shrivelled leaf had withered from emerald green to muddy brown.
- Fog filled the air.
- Thick fog, like a dense clammy blanket, hung in the air.

Independent work

- In the activity opposite, ask the children to look at the adjectives or phrases in bold and then find an alternative adjective or phrase from the box to substitute into the sentence.

Plenary

- Go through the activity orally as a class, or give the children the answers to self-correct. Encourage the children to suggest, or use a thesaurus to find, additional adjectives for some of the sentences.

Further support
- Remind the children to read the sentences, trying the different adjectives or phrases, instead of the ones in bold, until they find the most appropriate one.

Powerful adjectives

■ Find more powerful adjectives or phrases to put into these sentences.

> **glittering like gold**   **blazing**   **exhausted**   **parched**
>
> **ancient**   **like a wounded animal**   **gnarled**
>
> **like a white carpet**   **snaking**   **as clear as a bell**
>
> **full of beans**   **worn out**

1. The **old** tree with its **rough** bark looked strange in the twilight.

2. The snow, **all white**, lay glistening in the sun.

3. The **bright** sun shone fiercely on the **dry** ground.

4. The **old** shoes were only fit for the bin.

5. The **tired** footballers were shattered after playing extra time.

6. A button, **shining brightly**, could be seen on the floor.

7. She blew on the hot steam, **rising** from the coffee, before taking a sip.

8. He heard the noise **clearly**.

9. The boy, **upset**, lay crying on the floor.

10. The children, **excited and energetic**, were jumping about and fidgeting.

Singular or plural?

Objectives
Y3. T2. S4.
To extend knowledge and understanding of pluralisation.

Y3. T2. W11 & S5.
To use the terms 'singular' and 'plural' appropriately.

Guided work

1. Ask the children if they remember the word *plural*. What is the opposite? (Singular.) Reinforce that singular is one object or person, plural is more than one. Ask them for examples of words to which we add an *s* in order to make them plural and list these under the heading: *Adding s.*

2. There are many words that do not just add an *s* to make them plural. Write the words: *bus, dress, fox, potato.* Put the first word into a sentence, verbally, and ask the children to make it plural. Can they hear what ending makes the word plural. List these under: *Adding es.*

3. Do this again with the words: *mouse, man, woman, child, goose, tooth.* Take each word separately, as these have irregular plurals and do not fit into a pattern. Add the heading: *Irregular plurals.*

4. Write: *sheep, deer, salmon, fish.* Discuss the singular and plural of these words, which do not change. Add the heading: *No change.*

5. Write the following sentences on the board. Read the first sentence, asking the children to identify what is wrong. Ask a volunteer to correct the word. Work through the other sentences.

- The child were playing in the snow.
- When he went in he saw hundreds of mouse everywhere.
- It took four man to rescue the dog.

Independent work

● Copy the sheet opposite on to different coloured card for singular and plural, and cut out the cards. Shuffle the singular words as a pack and deal them to the players (in pairs/small groups). They spread them out face up in front of them, so everyone can see all the words. Shuffle the word ending/plural cards and put the pack face down. Each player takes a turn to put a correct word ending or irregular plural with any word they have. If the card they turn over is no use, they put it face up next to the pile in the centre. The next player can then choose that card or take the next card from the face-down pack. The winner is the player who gets all their plurals first. If the children can identify any of the plurals that are the same as the singular, they can keep the card.

Plenary

● Go through other sentences as you did during the lesson:

- The buses was picking up passengers.
- There were a few lovely dress in the window.
- I saw a foxes in the garden.

Further support
● Make a poster with the children of common words in the singular and plural, both regular and irregular. Simple pictures could be used to decorate it. Display it and refer back to it as the children work.

Singular or plural?

sheep	bus	goose	es
deer	dress	tooth	es
salmon	bush	s	es
fish	fox	s	es
car	potato	s	es
boy	tomato	s	es
shop	mouse	s	es
bike	man	s	es
toy	woman	es	es
book	child	es	es

Collective nouns

Objectives
Y3. T2. S4.
To understand the term 'collective noun' and collecting examples – experiment with inventing other collective nouns.

Further support
● Remind the children to read all the words in the box first. Then ask them to read each sentence saying the word 'something' for the blank space, and try to understand the meaning of each sentence before choosing the most appropriate collective noun.
● The lists of nouns could be displayed on the classroom wall. New collective nouns could be added as and when appropriate.
● Make up similar sentences with the children to use their suggested collective nouns, for example: *The (cuddle) of teddy bears was on the bed.*

Guided work

1. Before working on collective nouns the children should be familiar with common and proper nouns. If not, reinforce by teaching points 2 and 3 briefly first.

2. List some common nouns, for example: *dog, car, flower, boat, paper.* Read them and ask the children what we call these words, or remind them that these are nouns. Tell them that these everyday objects are called common nouns. Put this heading above the list.

3. List some proper nouns, for example: *Mickey Mouse, London, Buckingham Palace, April, Sunday.* Ask the children what sort of words these are, or tell them that these are also nouns but are special because they are particular people, places, dates or special objects. Tell them that these special nouns are called proper nouns. Put this heading above the list.

4. Play a word game with another sort of noun. Give the children a definition or show them a picture for each of the following collective nouns. As they suggest the answer make a list of the words: *choir, swarm, army, herd, library, party, family, flock, pride, bunch, gang* and *crowd.* Use picture cards or clues such as: *What do we call a group of people who sing together? What do we call a collection of books?* Explain that these are collective nouns because they are nouns that 'collect' the same kind of item together into one group. Write *collective nouns* above the list. Tell the children that collective nouns usually go with singular verbs, for example: *The bunch of bananas is on the shelf. A litter of puppies was in the basket.* Explain that it is often in this form: *A/The [collective noun] of [plural noun].*

5. Encourage the children to make up some of their own collective nouns for fun, for example: *a cuddle of teddy bears, a jam sandwich of cars, a snuggle of blankets.*

Independent work
● Ask the children to identify the collective noun which is the most appropriate in each sentence on the photocopiable sheet opposite. This can then be written in the space, or the words can be cut out and stuck in each sentence.

Plenary
● Briefly go through the activity orally.
● Use objects around the classroom or table to group with a collective noun: *pot of pencils, pile of books* and so on, or use picture cards again, especially those related to the sentences in the activity.

Collective nouns

■ Choose the most appropriate collective noun to fit in each sentence.

swarm	crowd	bunch	party	flock	army
herd	pride	gang	choir	library	family

1. My entire _____ is coming to the wedding.

2. I received a _____ of flowers yesterday.

3. My local _____ has thousands of books.

4. The _____ was coming into the barn for milking.

5. That _____ sings beautifully.

6. The _____ marched down the road.

7. There was a _____ of bees around the hive.

8. The school _____ went to the museum.

9. We were very lucky to spot a _____ of lions on the African plain.

10. The sheep dog was rounding up the _____ .

11. The _____ cheered as City scored.

12. The _____ of boys strolled past the chip shop.

What is a pronoun?

Objective
Y3. T3. S2.
To identify pronouns and understand their functions in sentences.

Guided work

1. Write some nouns on the board, for example: *chair, baby, rabbit, boy, car, children, Mrs Barber, the Lord Mayor* and so on. Ask the children if they remember what sort of words these are (nouns).

2. Now write these simple sentences on the board, underlining the main nouns:

- Mrs Barber has a blue coat.
- The car is red.
- The children went to the park.

Read each sentence with the children and ask them what the underlined words are.

3. Add these sentences to the board and read them out:

- The bus stopped but the people did not want to get on the bus.
- James and Carl have borrowed the ball from James and Carl's friend.

Tell the children that sometimes we can refer to things differently to make it simpler and less repetitive. Ask them if they can change anything to make the sentences read better:

- The bus stopped but the people did not want to get on it.
- James and Carl have borrowed the ball from their friend.

4. Tell the children that *it* and *their* are pronouns. We use pronouns to refer to a person, animal or object that we have mentioned before by name (the noun). Pronouns stop us from repeating ourselves. Brainstorm a list of common pronouns to display.

Independent work

- Ask the children to identify and write the appropriate pronoun above the main noun/s in the sentences on the photocopiable sheet. They may need to use one or two of the pronouns more than once.
- Alternatively, the activity can be used without giving the children the choice of pronouns in the box.

Plenary

Brainstorm to revise pronouns, adding any new ones to the list you made earlier. Ask volunteers to make up short sentences or phrases using the pronouns they suggested.

Further support
- Display some of the most common pronouns on the classroom wall with simple sentences showing how they can be used.
- Remind the children to read all the words in the box first. Then ask them to read the first sentence several times, each time substituting a different pronoun to see which is appropriate.
- When helping children edit their own work, ask them to think about using pronouns where appropriate.

What is a pronoun?

■ Change the nouns in bold into appropriate pronouns.

them	he	we	us	hers	they
their	him	her	his	it	she

1. **Angela** went to her friend's house for tea.

2. The dog jumped up at **Harry**.

3. The cat chased **the mouse**.

4. The clown gave each of **the children** a balloon.

5. **Daz and Bella** went to the match. Then Daz and Bella went home.

6. **Tim** went to see the doctor.

7. Jack went home in **Al's** car.

8. That book belongs to **Sharon**, not Toby.

9. Manny went to **Simon and Sally's** house.

10. This painting is **Fozia's**.

11. **Dan and I** boarded the train.

12. The tickets are for **Adam and me**. Can **Adam and I** have them please?

50 LITERACY HOURS FOR LESS ABLE
LEARNERS: Ages 7–9

Conjunctions and connectives

Objectives

Y3. T3. S5.
To explore how sentences can be joined in more complex ways by using a widening range of conjunctions.

Y4. T2. T20.
To use connectives of time.

Guided work

1. Make a chart of conjunctions, for example: *and, but, or, where, wherever, since, because, as, for, if, although, unless, than, like, as if, while, whereas, so that, in order that, such that, except, however, therefore, furthermore, additionally.*

2. Make a list beside it of time connectives, for example: *before, after, until, since, later, earlier, firstly, secondly* (and so on), *initially, then, just then, finally, shortly, afterwards, soon.*

3. Read the conjunctions with the children. Explain that they are used to join phrases or sentences together. Read the time connectives and explain that these are conjunctions that give us an idea of when something happens. Explain that using connectives can make writing flow better.

4. Write these sentences on the board: *The ice-cream fell on the floor. The girl knocked the ice-cream out of her brother's hand.* Then separately write: *The children were playing in the sea. A big wave made them run out quickly.* Ask the children how they would join the first two sentences into one, more complex, sentence. Then work with the second two sentences. (Answers will vary but could be: *The ice-cream fell on the floor <u>because</u> the girl knocked it out of her brother's hand. The children were playing in the sea <u>until</u> a big wave made them run out quickly.*)

5. Read the new sentences, after re-reading the originals, to show how the edited sentences read more fluently and give a more complete picture.

Independent work

● For group work, use the activity opposite as an oral exercise working with the children. This can be done with or without the suggested words in the box. Remind the children about changing or omitting words to make the sentences read fluently. Alternatively, this activity could be used on an interactive whiteboard for the children to manipulate the sentences.

● For pairs or individual work, ask the children to join the simple sentences together using the suggested conjunctions in the box.

Plenary

● Go through the activity orally taking any different suggestions into account. Reflect on whether different conjunctions or time connectives change the meaning of the text and explore whether the sentences still make grammatical sense.

Further support

● Display the chart of conjunctions and time connectives on the wall for the children to refer to. Add other words as appropriate.

● This may be a difficult exercise for some children, who may need plenty of adult support. Ask them to verbalise their ideas, trying different words, before changing the text.

● When helping children edit their own work, ask them to think about including conjunctions.

Conjunctions and connectives

■ Join the sentences by using an appropriate conjunction or time connective.

as	and	before	unless	secondly	however	as	if
but	because	therefore	so	since	afterwards	or	shortly

1. The boys were playing football in the park. _____ They went home for tea.

2. The baby was crying. _____ She was hungry.

3. Firstly you need to set out the game. _____ You need to decide who is playing.

4. I may go shopping. _____ I may go to the park.

5. The police cleared the area. _____ The fire crew started to put out the fire.

6. He felt tired after eating too much lunch. _____ He fell fast asleep.

7. The show finished at ten o'clock. _____ Many people went straight home.

8. I'm going to play outside. _____ If it starts to rain I'll go home.

9. This parcel was all battered when it arrived. _____ It had lost half its contents.

10. She walked down the road limping. _____ She had hurt her leg badly.

11. Dean had not been swimming. _____ He had lost his goggles

12. I had pizza to start with. _____ I had chocolate cake.

Prefixes

Objectives
Y3. T1. W10.
To recognise and spell common prefixes and understand how these influence word meanings.

Y3. T1. W12.
To use the term 'prefix'.

Guided work

1. Write these words on the board: *accurate, tidy, tasteful, starter, print, cook, change, freeze*. Discuss the meanings with the children.

2. Tell the children that the meaning of these words can be changed by adding a group of letters at the beginning of the word. Write these prefixes on the board: ex, *non, in, anti, mis, pre, un, dis*. Ask the children if they can remember what these parts of words are called (prefixes). Look at the word *prefix*, pointing out that *pre* is a prefix and means 'before'. So the word means fixing something on before (the word.) Encourage the children to tell you any other prefixes they know.

3. Work through the words in point 1, discussing which prefix is the most appropriate to add to each one. The words and prefixes could be put on to separate cards for the children to manipulate physically or this could be demonstrated on an interactive whiteboard.

4. As you do this, look at the meaning of the original word and the meaning of the changed one: accurate – exact, inaccurate – not exact; tidy – neat, untidy – not neat; tasteful – pleasing or beautiful, distasteful – displeasing or not beautiful; starter – someone beginning a race, non-starter – someone who does not begin a race; print – to type on paper, misprint – to type a mistake on paper; cook – to heat food, pre-cook – to cook earlier or before it is needed; change – make different, exchange – replacing something with something different; freeze – to turn to ice, antifreeze – a substance to prevent a car's radiator from freezing.

5. Discuss the meanings of the prefixes used: *in, un, dis, non, anti* – meaning 'not' or 'opposite'; *mis* – meaning 'wrongly'; *pre* – meaning 'before' or 'earlier'; *ex* – meaning 'out' or 'give out'.

6. Ask the children to suggest sentences to demonstrate how changing the words can give different meanings, for example: *The room was very tidy. The room was very untidy.*

Independent work

● Copy the sheet opposite on to card and cut into individual cards. Ask the children to read the words and prefixes, and then find the most appropriate prefix for each word to make new words.

Plenary

● Go through the activity orally, discussing the meanings of the original and the changed words.
● Alternatively, say a sentence, specifying a chosen word and ask the children for a prefix that changes the meaning of the sentence.

Further support

● The words and prefixes could be used a few at a time, asking the children to think of sentences in which to use the words first without, and then with, the prefixes. This could be written or done orally.
● This activity could be given a few cards at a time, for example: four or five of the words with the appropriate prefixes for them to make the words.
● Use Look-Say-Cover-Write-Check to practise spelling the words with their prefixes.

Prefixes

active	lead	in	mis
ability	take	in	mis
edible	sense	in	non
adequate	entity	in	non
happy	plus	un	non
disciplined	stop	un	non
bolt	tend	un	ex
dress	port	un	ex
appear	plain	dis	ex
content	press	dis	ex
trust	body	dis	anti
advantage	climax	dis	anti
place	dote	mis	anti
behave	septic	mis	anti

50 LITERACY HOURS FOR LESS ABLE LEARNERS: Ages 7-9

Suffixes

Guided work

1. Write on the board or interactive whiteboard: *thank, tender, enjoy, wasp, horseman, bright, use.* Discuss the meanings with the children.

2. Briefly recall the work on prefixes (see page 52). Then tell the children that we sometimes add on groups of letters at the end of a word, so that we can use the word in a different way. Write these suffixes on the board: *ful, ly, able, ish, ship, est, less.* Tell the children that these groups of letters can be added to the end of a word to change its meaning. Brainstorm any others the children know.

3. Work through the words in point 1, discussing which suffix is the most appropriate to add (some suffixes may fit comfortably with more than one word), for example: *thankful, tenderly, enjoyable, waspish, horsemanship, brightly, useless.*

4. Give the children a root word (for example, *hope*). Ask a volunteer to give the word plus a suffix (for example, *hopefully*). Then challenge the rest of the group to think of as many sentences as possible using that word. Repeat the game with different root words.

5. This is a difficult concept, but you may want to explain to the children that suffixes can change the work that words do in a sentence, for example: *The wasp was flying around* (*wasp* is a noun, the subject of the sentence). *Jan is very waspish today* (*waspish* is an adjective telling us that Jan is 'like a wasp' or 'spiteful' today.)

Independent work

● Give the children the word and suffix cards from the photocopiable sheet opposite. Ask them to read the words and suffixes, then to choose the most appropriate suffix for each word to make new words. Tell them that some suffixes may fit more than one word. Then ask them to use Look-Say-Cover-Write-Check to practise learning the words.

Plenary

● Go through the activity orally in a group, discussing the original and the changed words. Let the children experiment with putting them into sentences.

Suffixes

hope	owl	ful	ish
taste	sheep	ful	ish
wonder	relation	ful	ship
wish	friend	ful	ship
proud	companion	ly	ship
slow	hard	ly	ship
sad	fast	ly	est
bitter	clever	ly	est
drink	high	able	est
watch	soft	able	est
chew	home	able	less
like	humour	able	less
imp	heart	ish	less
child	shame	ish	less

What is an adverb?

Objective
Y4. T1. S4.
To identify adverbs and understand their functions in sentences.

Guided work

1. Write a list of verbs on one side of the whiteboard, for example: *jumped, crept, waved, travelled, trudged, went, spoke, laughed* and so on. List a selection of adverbs on the other side, for example: *quietly, rapidly, vigorously, loudly, grudgingly, silently, wearily, wildly.*

2. Point to the list of verbs as you read them. Ask the children if they remember what sort of words these are (verbs).

3. Point to the list of adverbs as you read them. Tell the children that these are adverbs and ask what they think their work might be in a sentence. The clue is in the word (ad-verb.)

4. Play with the list of verbs and adverbs to make short sentences and, where possible, ask the children to demonstrate the difference between the sentence with and without the adverb, for example: *They jumped. They jumped vigorously. She laughed. She laughed loudly. He spoke. He spoke quietly.* With each one point out how the adverb is telling us more about the verb. Underline the verbs in one colour and the adverbs in another.

5. Continue this with other verbs and adverbs that the children suggest. Demonstrate that the adverb does not always go next to the verb, but that it still tells us more about the verb, for example: *Slowly, the boy stepped across the rope bridge.*

6. Show the children that many adverbs end in the suffix *ly*, for example: *quickly, slowly, happily.* Point out the root words as you do this. There are some that do not, for example: *fast, soon* and *later*, and there are words that modify adverbs, for example: *quite, more* and *very.*

Independent work

● Ask the children to read the sentences on the photocopiable sheet opposite one at a time and try the different adverbs from the box to see which is the most appropriate one for each sentence before writing it in.

Plenary

● Go through the activity orally.
● Say a verb (or ask a child to) and brainstorm adverbs to go with it. Encourage volunteers to write these in a long column next to the verb on the board or choose and place adverb cards from a selection on an interactive whiteboard.

Further support
● Display a poster to tell the children that adverbs add detail to verbs.
● Remind the children to read the sentences before trying the different adverbs until they find the most appropriate one.
● If used interactively, the children can physically move the words into the sentences to experiment with how they read.

What is an adverb?

■ Put the most appropriate adverb into each sentence.

| well | lazily | contentedly | occasionally | eventually |

well   **lazily**   **contentedly**   **occasionally**   **eventually**

thoughtfully   **instantly**   **quickly**   **proudly**

heavily   **slowly**   **timidly**

1. The children ran _____ to the park.

2. The cat purred _____ when it was stroked.

3. The snail slithered _____ along the path.

4. _____ Tyrone went to United's games.

5. He worked on his homework _____ .

6. He behaved _____ when he had his operation.

7. _____ she went on to the stage to collect her prize.

8. He opened the door _____ , afraid of what he may find.

9. _____ Anna got out of bed and went for a wash.

10. She sat _____ on the chair and it broke _____ .

11. The burglar confessed to the crime _____ .

12. The snake swallowed the rat _____ .

50 LITERACY HOURS FOR LESS ABLE
LEARNERS: Ages 7-9

Familiar setting

Objectives

Y3. T1. T1.
To compare a range of story settings, and to select words and phrases that describe scenes.

Y3. T1. T11.
To develop the use of settings in own stories.

Guided work

1. Share the story extract on photocopiable page 108 with the children. Read the text through twice, then ask about the setting described, for example: Where do you think this story is taking place? How it is described? What words and phrases tell us about the setting? Are these words and phrases particularly effective or notable? Why do you think this? Who are the characters involved? How could the setting influence what happens to them in the story? Help the children to notice, as readers, how easily they can identify the setting and to be aware of this as they read the rest of the story and come to know the characters. It will be useful for them to bear this in mind when they write their own stories.

2. Brainstorm other familiar settings read in stories or ones the children have used in their own creative writing. Discuss why it may be easier to use a familiar setting when writing a story (it is sometimes easier to describe a place you already know; you can concentrate on imagining characters and events; readers similar to yourself will be able to identify and feel 'comfortable' with that setting, and so on).

3. Write one of the familiar settings just mentioned (for example, the classroom or the local park) on the board. Make it into a flow diagram as the children suggest some descriptive words and phrases that could be included in a description of the setting, for example: beautiful, colourful wall displays, bright sunlight. Move on to include story characters, such as a teacher and pupils. Consider together how the setting could affect the story, for example: Would the characters behave in a certain way because of their surroundings?

4. This could then be made into a short setting description or story opening as a piece of shared writing.

Independent work

● Give the children the photocopiable activity sheet opposite with the story extracts on photocopiable pages 108 and 109. Ask the children to compare the two extracts using the prompts on the chart. If they have time, encourage the children to list any other stories they know that also take place at home or at school.

Plenary

● Ask volunteers to share aspects of their comparison by reading them to the group and discussing the different interpretations.

Further support

● It may help some children to discuss each heading with a partner or in a small group before starting to write.

Familiar setting

Familiar setting	The Suitcase Kid	It's Not Fair
Setting		
Descriptive words and phrases used		
Characters involved		
What do you think about this description of the setting? For example: Is it a good description or not? Why do you think this? Is the setting described or just mentioned? How effective are the words and phrases used? Is it clear where the action takes place? Does it create a good picture in your mind? Why or why not?		

50 LITERACY HOURS FOR LESS ABLE LEARNERS: Ages 7-9

Fantasy setting

Objectives
Y3. T1. T11.
To develop the use of settings in own stories.

Y4. T2. T1.
To understand how writers create imaginary worlds.

Guided work

1. Read the story extract on the photocopiable sheet on page 110 with the children. Identify the setting and discuss how we know it is an imaginary place, for example: Which words or phrases tell us this? How does the description give you a picture of the setting?

2. Ask the children to suggest different imaginary or fantasy settings and describe what they are like, for example: a castle, a lost world, another planet and a fairytale land. Tell the children that good descriptions of setting use the senses to tell the reader what the place looks like, sounds like, smells like and how it feels to the characters.

3. Choose one of the settings (for example: a lost city) to describe and brainstorm descriptive words and phrases that could be used.

4. Ask the children to choose for whom the story is going to be written, by asking: What type of story is it going to be? Are you writing it to share with friends? Are you writing it for adults to read? Is it for younger children?

5. Use a planning form, such as the one opposite, to organise your ideas, explaining what you are doing as you write notes.

6. Using your plan, write the first draft of your story opening, or use the one suggested below. Explain to the children your thought processes as you write.

> I could see beautiful towers lit up beneath me. I swam towards them. I could see that they were brightly coloured with shimmering patterns everywhere. They looked like the gingerbread house in 'Hansel and Gretel'. As I moved between the buildings seaweed brushed my face making me shiver. Its strong smell made me feel sick. The water in this watery city felt much warmer. The place felt very welcoming. Then, above the sound of the water around my ears, I could hear a clanging noise. It sounded like the bell of a big clock striking far away in the distance.

Further support
● Children may find it easier to sketch the setting before describing it.
● Identify the type of setting that you want the children to write and then brainstorm and chart descriptive words and phrases to help with that particular setting.

Independent work
● Ask the children to plan and then draft a description of their own imaginary or fantasy setting using the photocopiable sheet opposite. The draft could be word-processed.

Plenary
● Ask one or two children to share their settings by reading their descriptions or planning notes omitting the title. Then ask the rest of the group if they can identify the setting.

Fantasy setting

Fantasy setting	For example, *The Lost City Under the Sea*
Audience	For example, *children my age*
Setting looks like: (where it is, objects/people/aliens around, colours, light, time of day/year)	For example, *beautiful towers lit up – beneath where I was swimming*
Setting smells like: (distinctive smells, unusual smells pleasant/unpleasant)	For example, *strong smell of seaweed – made me feel sick*
Setting sounds like: (quiet, noisy, nature sounds, voices, electronic)	For example, *clanging sound – like the bell of a big clock striking*
Setting feels like: (normal/strange, cold/warm, type of atmosphere)	For example, *seaweed brushed my face – making me shiver*

50 LITERACY HOURS FOR LESS ABLE LEARNERS: Ages 7-9

Setting in a different culture

Objectives

Y3. T1. T11.
To develop the use of settings in own stories.

Y4. T3. T2.
To read stories from other cultures.

Guided work

1. Read the story extract on photocopiable page 111 with the group and discuss how we know the setting is a different country or place from another culture. Consider where it might be (The Gambia). Talk about how the unusual sights are described and how it is this use of one of the senses that gives us a particular sense of place.

2. Consider how the setting is used in the story and how and why the characters react to their surroundings. Recall work on adjectives (see pages 40-43). Ask the children to imagine themselves in The Gambia.

3. Discuss different cultural settings and what they may be like, for example: a market in India, a rainforest safari, the frozen North. Then share the following extract (without the editing) with the children:

The Dance of the Chinese Lion
~~Chinese New Year~~
I was so excited, i   *The place was*
It was the first time I'd been to a Chinese New Year celebration. ~~There~~
heaving with people, most of them
~~were crowds of people. Most people were~~ speaking a language that I
                                        delicious
didn't understand. There was the smell of Chinese cooking and
unusual spices filling   *Drums began to beat*   *sleeping*
~~something else in~~ the air. ~~The drums were banging~~ loudly. The lion
   crouching   *stir. It raised its huge, decorated*
~~that was~~ on the ground started to ~~move. It lifted up its big colourful~~
              ,revealing all its vivid colours.   *strange, jerky*
head and stood up. It started to move around in a ~~funny~~ dance.
         enthralled at   *was so enchanted that*
Everyone was ~~really enjoying~~ the show. I ~~enjoyed it so much~~ I could

have watched it all night.

---

4. Explain that this is the first draft of a story opening and that they can help you edit it (or use the editing shown above). Remember to explain your thoughts, stating why you feel the changes are better (they are more precise, have more dramatic impact on the reader). Consider how long it should be, editing to reduce as well as improve.

Independent work

● Encourage the children to write and edit their own story opening using the photocopiable sheet opposite. Remind them to consider the audience and purpose for writing.

Plenary

● Ask one or two children to share their cultural setting (or part of it) by reading it to the rest of the group.

Further support

● Children may find it easier to sketch the setting before describing it.
● Identify the type of setting that you want the children to write and then brainstorm and chart descriptive words and phrases to help with that particular setting.

Setting in a different culture

Setting in a different culture	*For example, New Year celebration in China*
Audience I am writing for	*children my age*
Setting looks like: (where it is, unusual objects, people, light, time of day/year, climate colours)	*move around in a funny dance*
Setting smells like: (distinctive smells, unfamiliar smells, pleasant/unpleasant)	*the smell of Chinese cooking*
Setting sounds like: (quiet, noisy, nature sounds, voices, other languages)	*speaking a language that I didn't understand*
Setting feels like: (relaxed, friendly/ unfriendly, frightening and so on)	*enjoyed it so much I could have watched it all night*
Characters involved	*me, crowds of people, dancers*
What happens in the story	*an incident at the lion dance*

Myths, fables and traditional tales

Objective
Y3. T2. T9.
To write a story plan for own myth, fable or traditional tale.

Guided work

1. Read the extract on page 112 with the children. Tell them that this is a myth - an ancient story of gods or heroes. Discuss any difficult points of the story to make sure the children understand it. Show them the list of elements that may be included in myths from the sheet opposite and ask them to identify some of these in the story.

2. Share the stories on photocopiable page 113 and explain that these are fables, which are short stories that have a moral, giving us a lesson or advice on how to behave. Fables often have animals as the main characters that are given certain characteristics of people. Identify some of the elements of fables in the two stories.

3. Read the extract on photocopiable page 114. Encourage the children to identify the type of story. Tell them that a traditional or fairy tale is a story which includes elements of magic and magical or royal folk. Go through the story to identify some of the elements listed on the photocopiable sheet opposite.

4. Brainstorm a few ideas about writing a traditional story (or another genre) and record the ideas in plan form, for example:

Story title	Princess Tracy and the Three Wishes
Audience	classmates
Setting Main characters Words and phrases	palace, forest Princess Tracy, Prince Charming, fairy beautiful, tiny, forbidden, thick vegetation, gigantic, golden
Story opening Words and phrases	'Once upon a time...' Princess Tracy lonely in her new married life - Prince Charming away on royal business. Princess Tracy meets fairy bitterly unhappy, abandoned, listlessly strolling, appears
Middle (problem) Words and phrases	Fairy knows Princess Tracy is lonely; grants her three wishes - asks for: hobbies - too difficult - doesn't make her happy friends - they all start quarrelling - doesn't make her happy Prince Charming to come back home excited, magical, amazed, useless requests, in a blinding flash
Story ending (solution) Words and phrases	Prince Charming comes back home - business finished live happily ever after - promises never to go away again grand procession, triumphant homecoming, lost for words

Independent work

● Ask the children to plan a traditional tale, myth or fable to include some, or all, of the elements listed on the photocopiable sheet.

Plenary

● Ask one or two children to share their story plan with the rest of the group. Ask anyone who has planned a fable to give a synopsis and the moral to the story.

Further support
● Let the children plan in pairs to discuss their ideas.
● Help the children choose which type of story to write and give them quite a rigid planning structure.

Myths, fables and traditional tales

 Use the appropriate list to remind yourself about what you may want to include in your traditional tale, myth or fable.

Myths
- 'Long ago...', 'Before the world was...', 'On the island of...'
- Royalty, heroes, heroines, giants, strange creatures, gods, armies, animals
- Other lands (Greece, Australia, India, the Caribbean), mountains, the heavens, the underworld, seas, ships, mazes
- Tasks, quests, impossible challenges, punishments, puzzles, revenge, supernatural powers.
- Completion of deed or task, good triumphing over evil, or ending left open for a sequel.

Fables
- 'There was once a...'
- Animals and birds, animals talking and acting as humans, foolish people, wise people, few characters
- Streams or rivers, gardens, countryside, cottages
- Short, simple stories, very little detail or description in order to be memorable
- Challenge, tasks, confrontation, temptations
- Twist to the end of the tale, unexpected victory or ending, ends with a moral to the story.

Traditional tales and fairy tales
- 'Once upon a time...', 'In a land far, far away...', 'A long time ago...'
- Royalty, children, poor or rich people, fairies, dwarves, goblins or elves, animals acting as people, wicked stepmothers, fairy godmothers
- Palaces, castles, grand houses, cottages, forests
- Poisoning, imprisoning, spells, kidnapping, potions, things happening in threes, granting wishes, treasure and gold, magical objects, changing characters to objects or animals
- 'Lived happily ever after', marrying princes, death, punishment or banishment of evil characters.

50 LITERACY HOURS FOR LESS ABLE
LEARNERS: Ages 7–9

Sequencing

Objective
Y3. T3. T1.
To retell main points of a story in sequence.

Guided work

1. Cut out the pictures from the photocopiable sheet opposite or transfer it to an interactive whiteboard.

2. Explain to the children that you are going to help them sequence the narrative of a story before asking them to do it independently.

3. Remind the children of their work on comic-strip stories and speech bubbles (see page 32). Ask the children to look at each picture you have given them and discuss what is happening.

4. In pairs or small groups, ask the children to discuss and decide the order the pictures should be in to tell the story. Then discuss their sequencing as a group.

5. Ask the children either to create a simplified version of the story, noting what could be written beneath each picture, or relate the story orally in their pairs or small group.

6. Share some of the sequenced stories the children have ordered. Discuss how the reader can see the progress of the plot. How could they tell in which order the action was happening?

Independent work

● Give the children their own sets of pictures cut from an enlarged copy of the photocopiable sheet opposite. Ask them to add their own drawings to elaborate upon the story or work together to add details. They should then sequence the pictures in the correct order and glue them on to a sheet of paper, numbering the pictures in the correct sequence.

● Ask them to write captions.
● Once the sequence is established by the group, it could be written up in shared writing alongside the pictures, or the children could work individually.

Plenary

● Ask one or two of the children to retell the story by reading out their captions. Discuss any differences between the versions.

Further support
● Similar activities could also be done with giving just sentences to be sequenced rather than pictures (for example, simple versions of traditional tales). Children could draw their own storyboards to make the story sequence.
● Strips of simple sentences could be typed that tell the story. These could be given to individual children who need more help with this activity. Encourage them to read the sentences, with adult help if necessary, and sequence them along with the pictures.

Sequencing

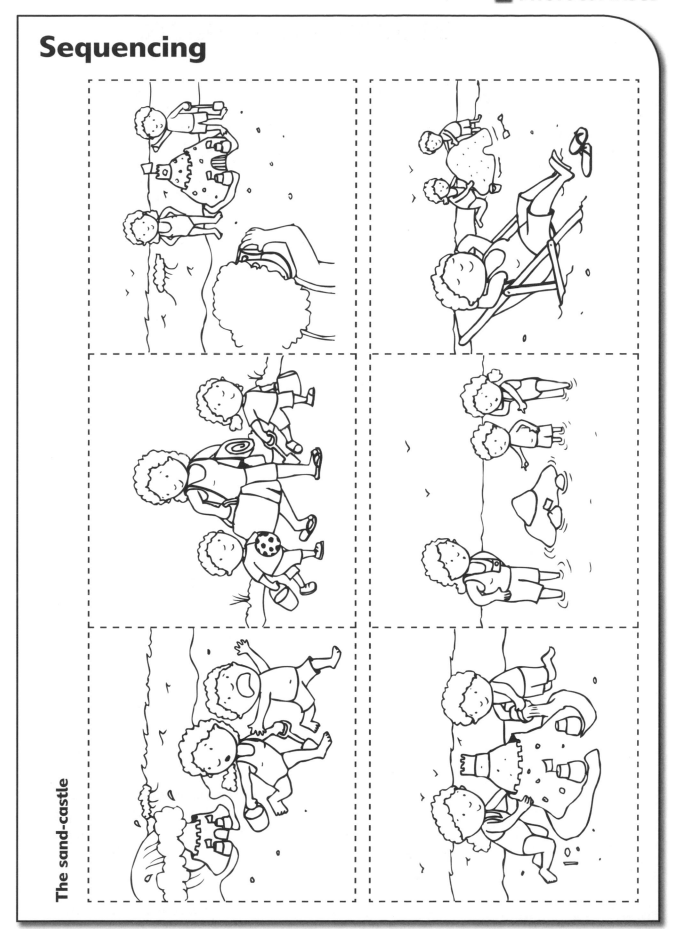

The sand-castle

50 LITERACY HOURS FOR LESS ABLE
LEARNERS: Ages 7-9

Building atmosphere

Objective
Y4. T2. T4.
To understand how the use of expressive and descriptive language can create mood, arouse expectations, build tension and so on.

Guided work

1. Read the extract on photocopiable page 115 and discuss how the text creates atmosphere and builds up to an exciting part in the plot. Notice how the use of adjectives and adjectival phrases contribute to making a vivid picture, for example: *the scent of danger*.

2. Write out the following text, leaving space between the lines. Explain that you are going to edit part of a story, focusing on the use of adjectives to contribute to the plot.

> The children trudged slowly up the mountainside. The three wanted to get to the top to see where Ryan had gone. As they climbed nearer the summit they could feel the cold air on their faces. They begin to worry about what had happened to Ryan. Had he fallen? Or was he just sitting there waiting for them? They would soon find out as they took their last steps to the peak.

3. Read the text and ask the children what it makes them feel. Can they picture what is happening? Does it make them want to find out more? Could it be better written? How could the description be more vivid. Draw out that using expressive and descriptive adjectives would make the picture in the reader's mind much clearer and more exciting.

4. Work through the text to include the children's suggestions of powerful adjectives to create mood, arouse expectations and build tension. The edited text could become something like:

> The anxious children, now exhausted, trudged slowly up the slippery, snow-covered mountainside. The three buddies desperately wanted to get to the top, which was hidden by thick cloud, to see what had happened to Ryan. As they carefully climbed nearer the summit they could feel the icily cold air freezing their already chapped faces. They began to tremble in fear when they thought what might have happened to Ryan. Had he plunged to his death? Or was he just sitting there waiting for them, having a laugh? They would soon find out as they took their final few steps to the isolated peak.

5. Read the edited text and compare its impact with the original.

Independent work

● Ask the children to read the text on the photocopiable sheet opposite and discuss with a partner adjectives and adjectival phrases that could improve the text. Ask them to record their ideas in the box before editing the text.

Plenary

● Compare a couple of edited versions read out by volunteers.

Further support
● Some children will need adult support in order to recognise adjectives and adjectival phrases. Tell these children the noun and ask them to use a word or phrase to describe it. For example, give the children the word *dog* and they could use *hairy, fussy, three-legged* and so on to describe it.
● Ask the children to compile a chart of the adjectives they used.

Building atmosphere

■ Brainstorm some adjectives and adjectival phrases and write them in the box. Choose some of them to include in the story below:

Sam woke up happy because it was his birthday. When he went downstairs his mum wished him a happy birthday then gave him a card and a small parcel. He opened it to find a book. Sam felt disappointed.

At school things didn't get much better. No one wished him a happy birthday and he got into trouble for frowning. At the end of the day he walked slowly home with a tear in his eye.

But when he finally got there and opened the door he just couldn't believe his eyes. All his family, friends and even his teacher were inside singing, 'Happy birthday to you'. Everyone was smiling and wearing party hats. There were balloons everywhere and a table full of sandwiches, crisps and cakes, with the biggest birthday cake he'd ever seen.

Then, his mum put her hand over his eyes and took him to the window. As she moved her hand Sam saw a new bike. It was just what he wanted!

The passing of time

Objective
Y4. T1. T3.
To explore chronology in narrative.

Guided work

1. Read one or two of the extracts on photocopiable pages 112, 114 and 116 and discuss with them how the authors have indicated when the story is set and any passing of time, for example: *Long, long ago, One day, A long time ago, then, now* and *just then.*

2. Brainstorm other indications of time and time connectives they could use, making a list of these on the board, for example: *before, next day, seconds later.* (Alternatively, use the one created for the lesson 'Conjunctions and connectives' on page 50.)

3. Discuss different types of story in which the passing of time might be significant, for example: *a diary format, time on a desert island, a ship's log, telling a story from the past, a time machine, remembering an event.* Remind the children about how time connectives (see page 50) can help readers appreciate the passing of time in a story.

4. Read the text below, without the italic text at first, and ask the children to suggest indications of time and time connectives (or use the phrases in italic). Re-read, and compare the two versions.

> *The next day* He awoke to find he was on a beach. *It must have been early morning as* The sun was *just beginning to shine* shining above the horizon. He remembered the horrible shipwreck *of the day before*. The sea must have washed him up here. He knew he must **spend the day** work***ing*** hard to find a way off the island. *First* He must explore the area to see what he could find. He set off *immediately* and walked all day long. When he returned to the same place on the beach again *as the sun went down* he sat down and ate some of the fruit that he'd found. *After the exhausting day* He fell straight to sleep.
>
> *The next morning* He awoke with more energy and started to try to light a fire with some of the wood that'd he'd brought back.

Independent work

● Ask the children to read the text on the photocopiable sheet opposite, then brainstorm with a partner suitable words to show the passing of time in the extract. Encourage them to edit the text.

● To challenge the children further, ask them to continue the story, remembering to indicate the passing of time where appropriate.

Plenary

● Invite one or two children to share their editing of the text and continuation of the story. Ask the children listening to say how much time has passed in the story.

Further support
● Display the chart of time connectives you made to help the children to express the passing of time.

The passing of time

■ Read the following extract. Brainstorm some words that indicate the passing of time and write them in the box. Choose some to include in the text. Then have a go at continuing the story.

Jane could not sleep. She decided to think about happy memories to help her nod

off, so she let her mind start to wander. She thought about when she had run in and

out of the waves with Jack, her big brother. They had been staying in a caravan by

the sea. The weather had been wonderful until they had that terrific thunderstorm.

She remembered her first visit to the bowling alley. Jack was really good and

knocked down many of the pins, but she could hardly lift the ball!

A character sketch

Objectives

Y3. T2. T8.
To write portraits of characters.

Y4. T1. T11.
To write character sketches, focusing on small details to evoke sympathy or dislike.

Guided work

1. Read the story extract on the photocopiable sheet on page 117 with the children and discuss how the character of Grandma is written, for example: *What do we find out about Grandma from this extract? What does she look like? How does she behave towards others? What words and phrases in the description help us to make a picture in our minds of Grandma?* Help the children to notice the details that the author includes to encourage dislike and humour from the reader.

2. Ask the children to suggest a few more words and phrases to describe George's grandma. What do they think it would be like to have a grandma like her?

3. Explain that you are going to work together to develop a character sketch. Discuss different character types and what they are like, for example: *family members, friends, dinner staff at school, the milkman, a bully, a burglar.* Ask them about the different personalities people have and remind them that there are lovely people and others who are bad or nasty. Tell them that you are going to plan the description of a person who is not very pleasant.

4. Ask the children to brainstorm a few suggestions of the sort of character you could describe to evoke dislike in a story reader, for example: *a bully, a mean neighbour, a burglar.*

5. Use the photocopiable sheet opposite to plan the sketch of your chosen character, for example, *a burglar* (some suggested details are included). Involve the children in suggesting details to add to the plan as you work through the form together step by step.

Independent work

● Give the children the activity opposite. Encourage them to work in pairs before planning their own character sketch to create a figure who evokes dislike in the reader, for example: a bully, a vandal, a conman, a hijacker, a car thief. How could this character be described? Remind the children that unpleasant characteristics could well be more than just physical. They may want to emphasise the 'acts like' over the 'looks like'. Their character could look perfectly normal but be a real meany!

Plenary

● Ask a volunteer to read the notes from their character sketch. Then ask another volunteer to draw a quick sketch of that person on the board. See if it ties in with how the author imagines the figure.

Further support
● Brainstorm useful words and phrases for describing an unsympathetic character and make a list of these for display.

A character sketch

Character sketch of	*For example, a burglar*
Audience I am writing for	*For example, everyone in the community – adults and children*
How do I want my audience to feel about my character?	*For example, dislike, worried, wanting him caught*
Character looks like: (eye colour, hair colour, size, expression)	*For example, beady eyes, huge muscles, unshaven*
Character wears: (jeans, jackets, shoes)	*For example, brown stocking over his face*
Character acts like: (mean, unhappy, rude to others)	*For example, aggressive, dangerous, may shoot anyone who gets in his way*

Writing a character sketch

Objectives
Y3. T2. T8.
To write portraits of characters.

Y4. T1. T11.
To write character sketches, focusing on small details to evoke sympathy or dislike.

Guided work

1. Re-read the extract on photocopiable page 117 to recall George's grandma, for example: how unpleasant she was to George so that he thought that she was selfish; her pale brown teeth and puckered up mouth. Then remind the children about the planning you did together for the character sketch of an unsympathetic story character (see 'Planning a character sketch' on page 72).

2. Explain that you are going to work towards writing the character sketch planned in the previous activity (page 72), making it into a wanted poster. Tell them that you want to create a poster that may help the police catch this dangerous burglar.

3. Discuss the audience that the poster will be written for, as this will affect the vocabulary used. Remind the children that, as the readers could be anyone in the area, both adults and children, the description needs to be clear and simple, as well as thorough.

4. Read the planning form you filled in together, then work with the children on the photocopiable sheet opposite. Ask the children to take turns in quickly drawing the burglar using the information given. The first child could outline the head, the second could draw the eyes, the third the nose and so on.

5. Refer to your planning notes to complete the character sketch, involving the children as you do this. Or, use ideas from this example:

> Trevor Takeall is a very dangerous burglar. He is about 30 years old, 6 feet tall and is very muscular. He has small beady eyes, a bent nose, a bald head and is usually unshaven. He has a tattoo of an anchor on his left forearm and 'LOVE' and 'HATE' on his fingers. He was wearing a black bomber jacket, blue jeans and trainers when last seen. He wears a stocking over his face when out on a job. Do not approach Takeall as he can be violent. He is armed and may shoot anyone who gets in his way. If you have any information about this man, please telephone 999 immediately and ask for the police.

Independent work

● Give the children the photocopiable sheet opposite. Ask them to use the planning that they did in 'A character sketch' on pages 72 and 73 and to write their character profile on the wanted poster, giving identifiable physical and social characteristics.

Plenary

● Ask one or two children to share their character sketch by showing and reading their posters to the rest of the group.

Further support
● Some children may find it easier to draw their character first, before trying to write their profile.

Writing a character sketch

■ Draw a picture of the character whose details you planned previously.

_____

■ Using the character sketch details you planned previously, write a description of your character.

_____

_____

_____

_____

_____

_____

50 LITERACY HOURS FOR LESS ABLE
LEARNERS: Ages 7-9

Using dialogue

Objectives
Y3. T1. W19.
To explore common vocabulary for introducing and concluding dialogue.

Y3. T1. S7.
To develop basic conventions of speech punctuation.

Y3. T3. S4.
To use speech marks and other dialogue punctuation appropriately.

Guided work

1. Read photocopiable page 118 and discuss, for example: *What is happening at the opening of this story? What happens to make Laura surprised?* Look closely at the words spoken and especially how the conversation is set out. Point out that a new line is used for each new speaker and that speech marks indicate what is actually said.

2. Ask volunteers to 'act' the dialogue.

3. Write the following text, or something similar, on the board.

> The boys were bored. The summer holidays were nearly at an end and they had done everything there was to do: been to the park; played on the computer; been swimming and played so much football they must have worn out a pair of trainers each. Dad, realising that they were at a loose end, came out into the garden and suggested a trip to Alton Towers.

4. Suggest that we would be able to identify with the characters more and the story would be more lifelike and immediate if the characters spoke to each other.

5. Work through the activity on the page opposite, identifying the characters and deciding who should speak, what they should say and the order in which they speak to each other.

6. Remind the children how to use speech marks and other dialogue punctuation appropriately.

7. Work through part of the text with the children, using the planning, to introduce dialogue into the text. Read the new version and compare its impact with the original. The text could have become something like:

> The boys were bored and they were grumbling.
>   'These summer holidays have been way too long,' moaned Daz.
>   'Yeah, we've done everything there is to do round here!' sighed Jason.
>   'We've been to the park, played on the computer...'
> Daz continued, chuckling, 'and we've been swimming and played so much football I reckon we've worn out a pair of trainers each!'
> Dad, realising that they were at a loose end, came out into the garden.
>   'How about a trip to Alton Towers?' he suggested.

Independent work

● Ask the children to use the photocopiable sheet to plan a piece of dialogue for their own story, or continue with the story drafted above.

Plenary

● Ask the children to read out their dialogue in pairs so that it is like a conversation or playscript.

Further support
● Display some dialogue on a poster to remind the children about speech marks and other dialogue conventions.

Using dialogue

■ Plan a piece of dialogue for a story.

Some alternatives to 'said'

uttered   exclaimed   whispered   asked   yelled   sighed

moaned   declared   revealed   groaned   replied   teased

joked   screamed   shouted   called   cried   suggested

Setting: where is the dialogue taking place?	*For example, in someone's garden*
Characters: how many, names, relationship between them	
Name of speaker: **Alternative word for 'said':** **Words spoken:**	
Name of speaker: **Alternative word for 'said':** **Words spoken:**	
Name of speaker: **Alternative word for 'said':** **Words spoken:**	
Name of speaker: **Alternative word for 'said':** **Words spoken:**	

Issues and dilemmas

Objective
Y4. T3. T11.
To explore the main issues of a story by writing a story about a dilemma and the issues it raises for the character.

Guided work

1. Discuss different issues and dilemmas that children may face, for example: *starting a new school, death of a pet, family break up.* Tell the children that these are very difficult things to talk about, but hearing and talking about other people's dilemmas (particularly in fiction) can sometimes help us to cope with our own problems.

2. Share photocopiable sheet on page 109, discussing the issue of someone small feeling that she cannot do things that the other children do and being bullied by others calling her names.

3. Choose a similar issue or dilemma to write about, for example: *a story about bullying*, as it can be a problem in school. Remind the children to consider the audience for whom you are writing and to be aware of how this affects the use of language.

4. Use the activity sheet to organise your ideas for a story involving an issue or dilemma. For example:

Dilemma or issue facing main character	bullying of main character (Lyndsey) by Sam and her gang
Main character/s involved	Lyndsey and Sam
Audience/reader	classmates
Story opening	Lyndsey is bullied by Sam after a class
Explanation of issue or dilemma	bullying started because Lyndsey told on Sam in class, now bullying all the time - getting Lyndsey on her own Lyndsey now very miserable - can't sleep or eat
Decision about issue or dilemma	has to make a decision about telling someone - who to tell: teacher, parent or best friend? what will happen if she tells? Bullied more/hated by other children/problem would be resolved what will happen if she doesn't tell?
Resolution	Lyndsey tells teacher teacher deals with Sam and gang - makes them understand bullying wrong and makes them apologise Lyndsey feels much better

Further support
● Make a list with suggestions from the children of words that might be helpful when writing about issues and dilemmas and display it for the children to refer to as they work.

Independent work

● Give the children the activity sheet opposite. Ask them to plan a story involving an issue or dilemma and begin to write it.
● Alternatively, let the children begin writing by making use of the planning form completed together in the main part of the lesson.

Plenary

● Ask one or two children to talk about the issue raised in their story and how they see it being resolved.

Issues and dilemmas

Dilemma or issue facing main character	
Main character/s involved	
Audience/reader	
Story opening (with introduction of issue or dilemma)	
Explanation of issue or dilemma (impact on main character)	
Decision about issue or dilemma (main character's decision about resolving problem)	
Resolution (dealing with issue or dilemma)	

50 LITERACY HOURS FOR LESS ABLE
LEARNERS: Ages 7-9

An introduction to plays

Objectives
Y3. T1. T15.
To write simple playscripts based on own reading and oral work.

Y4. T1. T13.
To write playscripts, for example using known stories as basis.

Guided work

1. Look at the pictures on a copy of 'Speech bubbles' on page 33. Use suggestions from the children to put words into the speech bubbles or use a comic strip that one of the children completed in that lesson.

2. Ask one child to play the princess and one to play the frog and to read the speech bubbles. Tell the children that this is like a little play because it tells a story through the words that the characters say to each other. However, the way it is written at the moment would be too difficult to act out.

3. Remind the children that plays are set out a certain way to make it easy for the actors to speak their lines and know how to behave on stage. Ask volunteers to read the parts in the playscript on photo-copiable page 119. Discuss the format and point out the use of small capitals and italic and that there is very little text that is not dialogue.

4. Tell the children that they can help you make the comic-strip story into a simple script. Work through the comic strip, putting down the spoken words and any stage directions in the correct format. Refer to page 119 as needed. Ask some of the children to act out the play. The play may be something like:

In a garden.
PRINCESS, *kneeling by pond playing with a ball. Ball bounces into pond.*
PRINCESS: Oh no, I've lost my golden ball. (*Begins to cry*)
FROG *jumps on to lily pad with ball.*
FROG: Is this why you're crying? (*Holding up ball*)
PRINCESS: My beautiful ball!
FROG: You can have it back if I can come and live in your palace.
PRINCESS: Yes, I'll do anything to get my ball back.
(*Exit* PRINCESS *followed by* FROG)
In the palace.
PRINCESS: Is there anything else I can do, dear Frog, to thank you for getting my ball back?
FROG: Yes, I would like a kiss.
PRINCESS, *reluctantly kisses* FROG *who changes into a handsome prince.*

Independent work

● Give the children the photocopiable sheet opposite and ask them to write the dialogue in the speech bubbles and then to begin work on changing the story into a simple playscript.

Plenary

● Ask some of the children to act out part of their plays for the rest of the class.

Further support
● Display an enlarged extract of the playscript to remind the children about the format.

An introduction to plays

■ What do you think these characters are saying? Write the words they say in the speech bubbles. Then change it into a simple playscript.

Writing a play

Objectives
Y3. T1. T15.
To write simple playscripts based on own reading and oral work.

Y4. T1. T13.
To write playscripts, for example using known stories as basis.

Guided work

1. Remind the children of the previous lesson when they made a storyboard into a simple playscript.

2. Ask for volunteers to re-read the playscript on photocopiable page 119. Discuss how a play tells a story through the actors talking to each other and that these words are written in a playscript with stage directions which set the scene and tell the actors how to behave.

3. Use the photocopiable sheet opposite to plan Scene 1 of a simple play based on a well-known story or traditional tale, for example 'Cinderella'. Recall the opening events of the story, the characters and any significant dialogue. As you work, remind the children that they are converting a narrated story into dialogue, so they need to always be aware of what the characters might say to each other.

4. Then begin to write this first scene as a playscript. Keep reminding the children about the presentation which makes it clear for the actors, including brief stage directions which help to set the scene and tell the actors when their characters are on stage, involved in the action. Write your own or it could begin like this:

> *In the kitchen.*
> CINDERELLA *in rags, dancing with broom. Enter* STEPMOTHER.
>
> **STEPMOTHER:** Get on with your work girl. Don't daydream about the ball because you're not going!
>
> **CINDERELLA:** Sorry Mother, but please could I go, I've finished all my work?
>
> **STEPMOTHER:** Certainly not! Wash the floor again!
>
> *Exit* STEPMOTHER. CINDERELLA *stands daydreaming. Enter* FAIRY GODMOTHER *waving her magic wand.* CINDERELLA *jumps when* FAIRY GODMOTHER *appears.*
>
> **CINDERELLA:** Oh! Who are you?
>
> **FAIRY GODMOTHER:** I am your fairy godmother and I have come to make sure you go to the ball.

5. Ask some of the children to act out the opening of the play.

Independent work

● Ask the children to plan the beginning of a familiar story, or one that they have written themselves, as the first scene of a playscript.
● Alternatively, ask the children to write the next scene of the example playscript on page 119.

Plenary

● Ask some of the children to act one or two scenes from their playscripts.

Further support
● Some children may find it easier to write a simple playscript from a storyboard, to reinforce the introductory work on writing plays.

Writing a play

	Set (where the scene takes place; props needed)	Characters (who is in each scene; where characters are on the stage)	Stage directions (how characters should act; entry and exit from stage)	Ideas for dialogue (useful words and phrases)
Scene 1				
Scene 2				
Scene 3				

Shape poems

Objective
Y3. T1. T14.
To invent calligrams and a range of shape poems, selecting appropriate words and careful presentation.

Guided work

1. Share the photocopiable sheet on page 120 with the children, reading the poems and asking the children what they notice about the shapes. Discuss the words that have been used in the poems as well as the shapes made. Do they think the poem being in a shape is better than just written as a 'normal' poem? Why do they think this?

2. Tell them that these poems are called shape or concrete poems because they take on the shape of the subject of the poem.

3. Ask the children for ideas of simple shapes that could be made into shape poems and ask them to draw one each, for example: *a snake, an elephant, a tree, a hand*. Share these drawings with the group.

4. Choose one of the shapes (for example, *a snake*), and ask the children to suggest powerful words which could be used in a poem about a snake, such as: *slithery, slimy, smooth, slinky, silky, wriggling, squirming, gliding, patterned, zigzagged, spitting, flicking.*

5. Make up a short, simple poem about a snake, set out traditionally:

> The slinky snake slithers –
> Silkily smooth.
> Tongue flicking quickly –
> Tasting the air.

6. Ask the children to draw a simple snake outline. Choose a child to copy their design on to the board, large enough to fit the lines of the poem into. Then write the poem into the shape, or ask a volunteer to do this. Compare it with the 'traditional' version. Do the children think the new one is more interesting, attractive and effective?

Independent work

● Ask the children to use the activity sheet opposite to plan a shape poem individually or with a partner, selecting appropriate words to use, and then write it out into its shape, taking care with the presentation.

Plenary

● Ask one or two children to read out their shape poem and display it to the rest of the group.
● Try reading the poems aloud while doing appropriate actions to fit the poems.
● Read out the poems as a choral speaking exercise.

Further support
● Identify a theme for the children to write about and, before they begin to plan their poems, brainstorm useful words and phrases connected with the chosen theme. List these and display them on a chart that they can see while they plan and write.

Shape poems

Ideas for poem (something which is a distinctive shape; there is plenty to describe)	
Useful words and phrases (appearance, movement; use of figurative language, rhyme)	
First draft of poem (set out as a poem is normally written)	
Ideas of shape or shapes to use for poem (sketch outline of shape the whole poem will take)	

Calligrams

Objective
Y3. T1. T14.
To invent calligrams and a range of shape poems, selecting appropriate words and careful presentation.

Guided work

1. Share photocopiable page 121 with the children, reading the poem and asking them what they notice. Point out significant words, particularly those in unusual print. Ask the children why they think these particular words have been typed differently. Do they like the effect?

2. Discuss the poem having individual words shaped so that they reflect what they mean, for example: *tall, thin, wide, dark.* Also look at the phrase 'curved as a wave' and ask the children what they think of it. Tell the children that these poems are called *calligrams* (from the word *calligraphy*: this means handwriting as an art). Explain the difference between calligrams and the shape poems the children created in the previous activity on page 84 (calligrams have individual words in them that are presented to reflect the meaning of that word rather than the whole poem shaped like its subject).

3. Write up some words that could be made to reflect their meaning, for example: *long, short, thin, thick, floating, high, down, loud, snaking, flat, wriggling, clouds, below, shivering, ghostly, happy, sad.*

4. Ask the children for ideas about how they would write some of these words to make them like little pictures suggesting the word meanings. Encourage volunteers to 'draw' their ideas on the board.

5. Choose some of their words to make into a simple calligram by sticking them on the board between written words that could form a line of poetry, as shown at the top of the page opposite. An interactive whiteboard would be ideal for this.

Independent work

● Ask the children to work in pairs on the activity opposite, presenting the poems as calligrams. Advise them to read each poem carefully first and notice the images that come into their minds.
● To challenge the children further, give them the poem from the lesson 'Shape poems' on page 84 and ask them to plan a calligram, selecting appropriate words to present pictorially. Encourage children to write it out, taking care with the presentation.

Plenary

● Display a few of the calligrams and ask everyone in the group to read them out one at a time with appropriate intonation, for example: *softly, loudly, quietly.*
● See if all the children have chosen the same words to represent pictorially and in a similar way.

Further support
● Brainstorm words that could be presented or written in a way appropriate to their meaning. List these and display them on a chart so they can be seen while the children plan and write.
● Share other calligrams such as *Rhythm Machine* by Trevor Harvey (from *Word Whirls*, 1998, Oxford University Press).

Calligrams

h
i
g
h in the sky

Clouds *floating*

a river *snaking* by

d
o
w
n below

■ Present these poems as calligrams.

The elephant trumpets,

His big ears flap.

Trunk curling up

Spraying water everywhere.

The beat is loud,

And then it's soft.

Ringing in my ear,

As the drumming dies away.

First it's round,

And then it's square.

Changes long and thin,

Then the bubble bursts. Splat!

Rhyming patterns

Objective
Y3. T1. T7.
To distinguish between rhyming and non-rhyming poetry and comment on impact of layout.

Guided work

1. Ask the children if they remember what makes words rhyme. If they need help identifying that rhyming words have the same sound at the end, say: *cake, fake, make, shake, bake, take, rake* and ask why these words rhyme.

2. Put the children into groups of three or four giving each group a different word (for example, *cat, pig, log, chop*) and ask them to think for a few minutes about words that rhyme with it. Encourage them to write the words down, not necessarily worrying about the spelling, and agree how many rhyming words they have found. The winning group is the one that can read out the most words that rhyme with their original word.

3. Share the photocopiable sheets on pages 122 and 123 with the children, reading the poems and discussing whether the poems use rhyme and, if so, what pattern of rhyme is used, for example: AABA – where the first two and the last lines rhyme, but the third line does not; ABAB – first and third and second and fourth lines rhyme; ABAC – first and third lines rhyme but second and fourth do not. Tell them that if poems use rhymes they are usually at the ends of lines. Remind them that poetry does not have to rhyme.

4. Choose which words at the ends of the lines rhyme and underline them. Let the children take turns to underline the rhyming words in a group situation, or they can work through the poems in pairs on their own copies.

5. Ask the children what they notice about the layout of the different poems. They may suggest: *different lengths of lines; one written in verses; one starting each line with a capital letter and the other not* and so on.

Independent work

● Hand out the photocopiable sheet opposite and ask the children to find a word to rhyme with the one underlined in each simple verse. Encourage the children to say each poem out loud and work out what ending sound they need for each rhyme.

Plenary

● Ask for a volunteer to read out their first verse, and then ask others to read out theirs, if they have used a different rhyme.
● Experiment with making nonsense verses by substituting a different word that either rhymes or does not. Do this with the other verses.

Further support
● Before the children start the activity, ask them to look at each poem and work out the rhyming pattern involved and discuss the different pattern in pairs or as a small group.

Rhyming patterns

■ Find rhyming words from the box to make these little verses rhyme:

drain	boat	blue	brain	say	goat	gate
glue	Sue	moon	train	boot	soon	skates
coat	stars	zoo	rain	fair	air	cars
hare	bars	hood	June	jars	away	mates

1. As I was sailing in my <u>boat</u>,

I saw a donkey in the street.

I looked again and saw a _____,

Chasing it around a seat.

2. As my ring went down the <u>drain</u>,

I began to fret

'Cos looking up I saw the _____

And knew my ring was gone.

3. I love to go round to the shop,

To see the sweetie <u>jars</u>.

Then I spy my very best,

The little sugary _____.

4. I love to roll around the streets,

On my roller <u>skates</u>.

I play like this all on my own,

But better with my _____.

5. High in the sky,

Bright shines the <u>moon</u>.

But morning is coming,

Soon, very _____.

6. I work so hard,

Thoughts in my <u>brain</u>.

It's all clear now,

The picture's a _____.

7. It runs and jumps

Up in the <u>air</u>.

Is it a rabbit?

No, it's a _____.

8. 'It should be <u>blue</u>.'

I hear her <u>say</u>.

'I'll fetch the _____

And stick _____.'

Water poems

Objective
Y4. T1. T14.
To write poems based on personal or imagined experience, linked to poems read.

Guided work

1. Share photocopiable page 124 with the children. Read and enjoy the poems and ask what they have in common, for example: *Do the poems rhyme? Do they have rhythm?* Discuss some of the evocative words and phrases used. Ask which poems the children like and why.

2. Tell the children you would like their help to write a water poem. Discuss what aspect of water to write about, for example: *A waterfall, because I like to watch how the water splashes down over the rocks.*

3. Model how to consider the audience, for example: *Is it a poem for my own pleasure? Is it to be included in a class anthology? Shall I write it for younger children?* Agree on a target audience.

4. Use the planning form opposite to organise your ideas, involving the children as a shared writing experience.

5. Using your plan, write the first draft of your poem. Explain to the children your thought processes as you write, for example: *I think I'll use the word 'drips' because the word seems to make a sound, so I can start 'The water drips and dropped'.*

6. Then model editing your first draft. Remember to explain your thought processes as you refine the text, looking for improvements to the sounds of the poem and the picture created.

Independent work

● Give the children the photocopiable sheet opposite. Encourage them to plan a poem, either about water or any other subject, and then to write their own poem using the planning. If possible, encourage them to type the first draft of their poem on to the computer to make the editing process easier.

Plenary

● List some of the 'watery' words and phrases the children have put on their planning forms and find rhyming words for these, for example: *splish/splash, soak/joke, dripping/dropping, spray/away.*
● Ask one or two children to share their poems by reading them to the rest of the group or class.

Further support
● If all the poems are to be on a similar theme (for example, *anything to do with water like rain, having a bath, swimming, rivers, waterfalls, the sea, a lake*), brainstorm useful words and phrases that would be appropriate. Make a list of these to display while the children are writing their poem.

Planning a poem on a theme

◾ Complete this plan to help organise your poem.

Subject of poem	
Title of poem	
Audience I am writing for	
Ideas for content of poem (main idea of poem, other details to include)	
Useful words and phrases (linked to title and subject of poem, powerful adjectives and verbs)	
Rhyming words (other words that rhyme with the useful words)	
First draft of poem (remember to leave blank spaces between the lines ready for editing)	

**50 LITERACY HOURS FOR LESS ABLE
LEARNERS: Ages 7-9**

Fact and fiction

Objectives
Y3. T1. T17.
To understand the distinction between fact and fiction. To use terms 'fact', 'fiction' and 'non-fiction' appropriately.

Y4. T1. T19.
To understand and use the terms 'fact' and 'opinion' and begin to distinguish between the two.

Guided work

1. Give each child three cards with *fact, fiction* or *opinion* on them.

2. Ask the children if they can explain what *fact* means (a fact is something that is true and can be proven). Ask them to suggest a few facts or give them some examples, for example: *dogs are animals, elephants can not jump, steel is a type of metal*.

3. Do the same with the word card *fiction*. Tell them that fiction is a statement or 'story' that is invented or created from imagination. It is not 'true'. Tell them that most of the stories we read are fiction. Ask them to suggest a few examples of fiction, for example: *the cat walked down the road with her shopping bag, the children started to eat the gingerbread house*. Tell them that it is confusing, but sometimes stories (fiction) can be based on facts!

4. Repeat this for the word card *opinion* (a belief or point of view held by a person or a group of people, which may or may not be true). Ask the children to suggest a few examples of opinion, for example: *I believe in ghosts; We think Beckham is the best footballer*.

5. Write *non-fiction* on the board. Tell the children that texts that are not fiction (a made-up story) are referred to as non-fiction. We call books that tell us facts non-fiction, for example: *biographies, information books, encyclopedias*.

6. For each sentence, ask the children to discuss with a partner and then hold up the card showing whether they think the sentence is fiction, fact or opinion:

- Dogs like to gnaw on bones.
- I think this is the best class in the school.
- Most children aged ten go to a primary or junior school.
- Darren woke up to find it had all been a dream.

Independent work

- Give the children the phocopiable sheet opposite and ask them to complete activity (a).
- As an extra challenge, give the children activity (b) and ask them to complete it.

Further support
- Make a poster showing the words *fact, fiction* and *opinion* with their meanings and give simple examples of each. Display for the children to see as they work.

Plenary

- Invite the children to think of their own sentences of fact, fiction or opinion to ask the rest of the group. The children can hold up the cards they used at the beginning of the lesson, showing whether they think each sentence is fact, fiction or opinion.

Fact and fiction

Activity A

◀ Are these fact or fiction?

1. A is the first letter of the alphabet in the English language. _____

2. The children found themselves in a magical forest. _____

3. People often wear glasses if they cannot see very well. _____

4. Most people in England live in houses. _____

5. People can travel in cars, on buses, in trains and by aeroplane. _____

6. When the spaceship landed strange creatures got out. _____

7. Maria Mouse put on her coat before going to buy some cheese
   for her baby mice. _____

8. Eleven people play in a football team. _____

9. Trains travel on railway tracks. _____

10. The prince and princess married and lived happily ever after. _____

Activity B

◀ Are these fact, fiction or opinion?

1. I believe that the world is a very big planet. _____

2. Deserts are usually hot, sandy places. _____

3. Charlie the car winked at his friend Billy the bus. _____

4. The toys all rushed into the toy box before Ali
   came into the room. _____

5. I think that United will win the cup. _____

6. The elephant is the largest animal on land. _____

7. Eleanor grabbed hold of the horse's mane as it galloped up
   towards the moon. _____

8. I think I will go to the park this afternoon. _____

9. The four seasons are spring, summer, autumn and winter. _____

10. We should not be in this attic. _____

50 LITERACY HOURS FOR LESS ABLE
LEARNERS: Ages 7-9

Non-chronological reports

Objective
Y3. T1. T23.
To write simple non-chronological reports from known information.

Guided work

1. Tell the children the distinctive features of non-chronological reports:

- They have a short paragraph introducing the subject.
- They are not in a time sequence.
- They give information – factual, not imaginative.
- They are written in the present tense.
- They are written in a formal way.
- They are organised into main ideas with supporting details.

2. Share the photocopiable sheet on page 125 with the children, reading the report and discussing it. Ask the children: *What is the report about? How is it organised?* Point out that the fact sheet has a short introductory paragraph and that it uses subheadings, in this case worded as questions, which indicates the main point discussed in the paragraph. Remind the children about paragraphs each having a main idea and supporting details.

3. Remind the children that it is important to organise information before writing a non-chronological report, and that we do this by sorting the information into a few main ideas or statements each with supporting details.

Independent work

- Give the children the photocopiable sheet opposite and ask them to cut out the sentences and sort them into three groups: *Food, Where they live,* and a third for those sentences which do not seem to fit in the other two. Then ask the children to discuss and identify the three sentences which state the three main ideas and put them at the top of the group, arranging the others in an order that they think makes sense. Ask them to draw three large boxes on a sheet of paper and stick the sentences down into the three boxes as though they were paragraphs, starting with the sentence which contains the main idea in each case.
- As an extra challenge, ask the children to use the information from the activity to write a non-chronological report in their own words. Suggest that they make notes on a topic that interests them, organise them in the same way, and then write a report.

Further support
- This activity could be made simpler by using just a selection of the sentences.

Plenary

- Discuss how the children sorted the sentences, asking them to justify their decisions. From this, see if any subheadings can be generated to further organise the report.

Non-chronological reports

■ Read and cut out these sentences.
Organise them into a non-chronological report.

They need straw, sawdust or something similar to sleep on.

It is very important to care for your rabbit to keep it in good condition.

Take care to keep all doors shut so your house rabbit does not escape.

Most rabbits live outside in a hutch, which is made of wire and wood.

Rabbits need a balanced diet to keep them healthy.

Rabbits can develop overgrown claws from not exercising on a hard surface.

Rabbits can eat moist food, such as fresh vegetables and fruit.

Rabbits should be brushed about once a week.

Overgrown claws can be dangerous because they curl over.

Rabbits need to have fresh water to drink.

If you have a house rabbit, hide electric wires or it may chew them.

Rabbits can live in hutches outdoors or indoors as house pets.

Rabbits can get overgrown claws caught in cracks.

Overgrown claws can be clipped carefully with normal nail clippers.

A popular way to keep rabbits now is in the house.

Sequencing instructions

Objective
Y3. T2. T14.
To appreciate how written instructions are organised.

Guided work

1. Remind the children that instructions tell us how to do or make something, how to play a game or get to a particular place and so on.

2. Display photocopiable page 126 and discuss the sequence words, numbering, verbs and layout.

3. Remind the children that verbs are important in instructions as they tell the reader what to do and how to do it. The verbs used in instructions give a command or order (the imperative form of the verb) directly to the reader, for example: *follow the road on the right* (in directions); *move back six places* (instructions for a game); *pour the milk in the pan* (cookery instructions).

4. When we use instructions, we need to give a logical sequence of commands that the reader can follow. Point to the instructions on page 126 and say to the children: *Imagine how lost Auntie would get if the directions on the page weren't in order!*

5. Write these sentences on card or on an interactive whiteboard so that they can be moved around independently:

- Use a teaspoon to take the teabag out of the mug.
- Add milk and/or sugar and then stir the tea.
- Boil the kettle.
- Pour the boiling water on to the teabag in the mug.
- While the kettle is boiling, put a teabag in a mug.
- Fill the kettle with cold water.

6. Discuss what these instructions are for. Ask the children if they can see anything wrong, and ask what would happen if they tried to follow these instructions to make a mug of tea!

7. Invite the children to work in pairs or small groups and decide the order that the instructions should be in. Then ask for volunteers to sequence the instructions into a logical order.

Independent work

- Give the children the photocopiable sheet opposite and invite them to read and then cut out the instructions, then sequence them logically and glue them onto a sheet of paper in the correct order.

Plenary

- Ask the group to help you to work out a simple list of directions, for example: how to get from school to the local shop.

Further support
- Select only six, seven or eight of the instructions for the children to sequence, as long as they make sense as a sequencing activity!
- Some individuals may require adult support to help them to read the sentences and think logically in order to sequence.

Sequencing instructions

■ Cut out and put this list of instructions into a logical sequence.

When the eggs are beaten, pour the oil into the frying pan.

When the frying pan is off the heat fold the cooked omelette in half.

Finally, before eating add a little salt and pepper.

Beat the eggs with a whisk or fork for a few minutes.

Place the frying pan on to the lit cooker ring.

Stir the mixture over the heat until the eggs start to set.

Lift the folded omelette on to a plate.

First crack two eggs into a bowl.

Take the omelette off the cooker and turn off the ring.

As the eggs begin to set, stop stirring and leave on the heat for a few minutes.

When the oil is in the pan, light the cooker ring and turn down low.

Pour the eggs into the frying pan that is on the cooker ring.

Writing instructions

Guided work

1. Recall things that you could give instructions for, for example: *directions from one place to another, playing a game, a recipe*. Then tell the children that you are all going to make a class cookery book, and are going to write instructions for making a sandwich.

2. Decide with the children who the cookery book will be aimed at, for example: *Will the book be to use in the class? Are the recipes for the cookery book for infants? Is the book for adults?* Ask the children to discuss this and consider what recipes would be appropriate for the audience for whom they have chosen to write.

3. Share photocopiable page 126 to remind the children about the importance of sequencing and imperative verbs in instructions.

4. In shared writing, use the scaffold opposite to organise the recipe writing. The instructions could be something like this:

How to make a cheese sandwich

Ingredients	Equipment
Two slices of bread	A plate
A small piece of cheese	A knife
Butter or margarine	A cheese grater

Method
1. Place the two slices of bread on the plate.
2. Spread the margarine or butter on one side of each slice.
3. Grate some cheese on to one slice.
4. Put the other slice on top of the grated cheese.
5. Cut the sandwich into squares or triangles.

Independent work

● Ask the children to use the photocopiable sheet to plan and then write their own simple recipe, for example: *making a cup of tea or coffee, beans on toast, a different kind of sandwich*. Encourage the children to type their recipe on to the computer, with the aim of compiling them into a class recipe book.

Plenary

● Ask one or two children to read their recipe to the rest of the class, perhaps while another child mimes the action for each step.
● Alternatively, use someone's recipe to make a cup of tea or coffee. Share a published cookery book with the children to look at the presentation in preparation for making a class cookery book.

Further support
● Make a list of imperative verbs that could be useful in recipes, for example: *beat, spread, mash, dice, grate, simmer, peel* and so on. Read the list with the children, add any other suggestions and then display it while the children are writing.

Writing instructions

Title of recipe
How to make a

Ingredients
(include how much of each ingredient)

Equipment
(kitchen utensils needed)

Method
(what to do; sequence of what to do first, second, third and so on.
Remember to use imperative verbs)

1.

2.

3.

4.

5.

6.

7.

8.

50 LITERACY HOURS FOR LESS ABLE
LEARNERS: Ages 7–9

Letter to an author

Objective
Y3. T3. T20.
To write letters using appropriate style and vocabulary for the intended reader.

Guided work

1. Ask the children if they have sent or received letters recently. Discuss some of the reasons we write letters, for example: to give news to a friend, to say thank you to a relative, to complain, to order something. Suggest, for example: *I've just read an excellent book and would like to write and tell the author how much I enjoyed it.*

2. Consider who will read the letter. Should it be formal or informal?

3. Show the children an example of a letter and discuss the format. Point out that it is directly addressed, in the second person, to the person reading it.

4. Use the planning form to organise your ideas. Pay particular attention to explaining the format of the letter. Tell the children that when a letter begins *Dear Mr, (Mrs* or *Ms)* it should end *Yours sincerely.*

5. Write the first draft of your letter, or use the one below. Explain your thought processes as you work.

> (address)
> (date)
>
> Dear Ms Wilson,
>
>   My name is _____ and I have just read your book *The Suitcase Kid* and I enjoyed it so much that I wanted to write and tell you.
>   I think the main character is very life-like and I love the way she keeps Radish the Sylvanian rabbit with her all the time. I think she needs him because her life changes so much and she isn't happy.
>   The book made me laugh and cry. I also thought having the alphabet to begin each chapter was a very original idea.
>
> Yours sincerely,

6. Model editing your first draft to correct and improve the letter. Explain to the children that the letter should sound polite but friendly, avoid repetition, and sound clear and interesting. Re-read the edited version and check all the children are happy with it.

Independent work

● Ask the children to plan and write their own letter to an author about a book they have just enjoyed.

Plenary

● Ask groups of children to compose a response to one of the children's letters.

Further support
● Display an enlarged copy of a fairly informal letter, or a completed draft of the one you have modelled, to remind the children of the format while they are writing.

Planning a letter

Address (writer's address written on the right) **Date** (under address)	
Dear..., (written on the left)	
Content of letter (brief introduction) (give information, opinion or recount event) (draw letter to a close)	
Conclusion (for example, *Lots of love* to a very close friend, or *Yours sincerely*)	

Writing a formal letter

Objective
Y3. T3. T20.
To write letters using appropriate style and vocabulary for the intended reader.

Guided work

1. Remind the children about the different reasons for writing letters and who they are written to. Then tell the children that you want to write a letter of complaint, for example: *I've just had a new fridge delivered and the door is damaged.*

2. Consider who the letter is for and what tone should be used, for example: *Is it a friendly or a stern letter? Is it formal or informal?*

3. Ask the children if they remember the format of a letter. Remind them that there are a few ways of presenting letters depending on how formal they are. If possible show them an example or two of a formal letter and discuss the details of presentation and vocabulary.

4. Use the scaffold opposite to write the first draft of a letter of complaint. Explain to the children what you are doing, pointing out which box to put your address in, which box to put the address of the person to whom you are writing and so on. Pay particular attention to explaining the format of the letter as you plan. Tell the children that the usual ending when a letter begins *Dear Sir or Madam* is *Yours faithfully*, You could include details such as:

> Further to my recent phone call, I write to complain about the damage to the door of my new fridge which was delivered yesterday. I was asked to put this in writing after my telephone conversation late yesterday afternoon.
>
> I was out when the fridge was delivered, so I was unable to unpack it until I returned home from work. This was when I discovered it had a very large dent near the top of the door. I feel very strongly that the damaged fridge should be replaced as soon as possible.
>
> I look forward to a prompt and satisfactory reply.

5. Edit your first draft if necessary. Stress to the children the importance of giving a full and accurate account and a polite but expectant ending.

Independent work

● Ask the children to work in pairs or individually to write their own letter using the photocopiable sheet opposite. They could complain about something that is damaged, or a wrong delivery, or not being able to see at a football match. If possible, encourage them to type their final draft on to the computer.

Plenary

● As a class, compose a reply to one of the letters the children have written apologising for the problem and offering a solution.

Further support
● Display an enlarged copy of a formal letter, or a completed draft of the one you have modelled, to remind the children of how a formal letter differs from an informal one.

Writing a formal letter

My address

Their address

Date

Dear Sir or Madam

Content of letter
(brief introduction)

(give information, outline complaint, give opinion, recount event, use formal language)

(draw letter to a close, for example: *I look forward to a prompt and satisfactory reply.*)

Signature (Yours sincerely or Yours faithfully

Explanatory texts

Objective
Y4. T2. T25.
To write explanations of a process, using conventions identified through reading.

Guided work

1. This activity involves identifying the features of explanations and format they usually take. Use the following list as a poster:

Texts that explain usually include:

An **opening paragraph** that
● begins with a definition of what the text is about
● says a little bit about the subject.
The main text
● first paragraph - describes *what* the subject is in more detail
● second paragraph - describes *how* the process works.
A **concluding paragraph**
● summarises what the text is about
● it may evaluate the subject or the effects of the process
They often also include **diagrams**.

2. Read photocopiable page 127 with the children. Compare it to the poster by asking them things like: *Is there an opening paragraph? What is the definition of the subject? Does it include diagrams?*

3. Tell the children that explanatory texts are usually written in a certain way. Work through the text looking for the following features. Use a different coloured pen to underline different features:

● Mainly uses the present tense.
● Usually written in a formal, impersonal voice.
● Uses factual material and may have technical language.
● Uses sequencing language to describe a process.
● Uses cause and effect language to describe a process, for example: *as a result, consequently, since, then, because, if, so.*

Further support
● Some children may find it easier to do simple diagrams before starting to write their explanatory text.
● Alternatively, children could record their explanatory text onto a cassette, after making notes to help them.

Independent work

● Give the children the planning form and ask them to work in pairs or individually to plan an explanatory text. Encourage them to describe something which is very familiar to them, for example, how and why they clean their teeth. After planning, encourage the children to write up their explanatory text, including diagrams if helpful.

Plenary

● Play a game of verbal 'Consequences' where the children take it in turns to add the next thing in a sequence explaining a process, for example: *the process of getting up and going to school.*

Explanatory texts

Subject of text	
Audience	
Opening paragraph (begin with a summary of what you are writing about)	
Main text (first paragraph – describe what the subject is in more detail) (second paragraph – describe how the process works)	
Concluding paragraph (summarise you may evaluate the subject or the effects of the process)	
Diagrams (these may be useful to show certain points)	

Persuasive writing

Objectives
Y4. T3. T23.
To present a point of view in writing, linking points persuasively and selecting style and vocabulary appropriate to the reader.

Y4. T3. T25.
To design an advertisement.

Guided work

1. Ask the children where they see or hear advertisements, for example, television, radio, posters, newspapers and magazines. Ask the children which advertisements they like and why, or at least which they remember and so are effective.

2. Discuss what advertisements aim to do (usually persuade people to buy a product). Tell the children that you are going to try to persuade them to buy something, for example, a new brand of toothpaste.

3. Read photocopiable page 128 with enthusiasm, in the way it may be performed on television or radio (or encourage volunteers to do this). Display the following list of typical features and ask the children which they notice.

- Opening grabs the attention – possibly a rhyme or jingle.
- Asks a question to make the audience think about what they need.
- States or claims something about the product.
- May include cause and effect, for example: what will happen if they buy or do not buy.
- Punchy conclusion, restating the main selling point of the product.
- Possibly a repeat of rhyme or jingle from opening.

4. Use the photocopiable sheet opposite to organise your ideas ready for writing. Ask: *What words and phrases would make my audience listen to this advert? Can I use rhyme to help me sell my product?*

5. Decide what type of advertisement you are going to write (such as for a newspaper or radio script) for a chocolate-tasting toothpaste.

7. Work with the children to write the advertisement. Remind them they are trying to influence people so the advertisement should use powerful words to describe why it is special:

Independent work

- Ask the children to work in pairs to create an advertisement for television or radio. Advise them to invent a new spin on something that is familiar to them. The advertisement could then be taped or videoed and played to the rest of the class.

Further support
- Suggest powerful, positive words appropriate to the children's products.

Plenary

- Ask for volunteers to perform their television or radio advertisement or share their advertising poster. Do a survey to see how many children would be persuaded to buy the product.

Persuasive writing

Name/logo

Catchphrase/jingle

Buyer/audience

Adjectives that 'sell' the product

Sketch of product

Other notes to persuade (why product is needed, why it is better than others)

Brief conclusion/repeated jingle

THE SUITCASE KID

I stopped yelling and started happily slurping my way through an ice cream. Mum and Dad had an ice too, and we all went for a little walk in the sunshine. And that was when we saw it. The cottage at the end of the road. A white cottage with a grey slate roof and a black chimney and a bright butter-yellow front door. There were yellow roses and honeysuckle growing up a lattice round the door and the leaded windows, and lots of other flowers growing in the big garden. In the middle of the garden was an old twisted tree with big branches bent almost to the ground. Mum and Dad were so taken by the cottage that they'd stopped keeping an eye on me. I toddled through the gate and made for the tree because it was studded all over with soft dark fruit. I picked a berry and popped it in my mouth. It tasted sweet and sharp and sensational. My very first mulberry. There was a For Sale notice on the fence. It seemed like we were meant to buy Mulberry Cottage. It wasn't quite in the country. It turned out to have a lot of dry rot and woodworm and for the first year there was dust everywhere and we couldn't use half the rooms. But it didn't matter. We'd found our fairy-tale cottage.

Jacqueline Wilson

IT'S NOT FAIR!

Kitty was the smallest girl in her class. Usually she did not care. She could swim well, and run as fast as most people – well, almost – and once came first in the egg and spoon race on Sports Day. So it did not matter – being small. That was what Kitty thought.

But one day something happened to make her change her mind. It was one of those days when nothing went right.

First of all, there was a new boy in Kitty's class. His name was Tom, and he was very, very tall. Kitty didn't like him very much, because he called her 'Shrimp'.

The whole class was working on a mural in paint and cut-out paper, and on this day Kitty and Tom and two other children were chosen to do special extra work on it.

Kitty was very excited. She loved painting – especially when you could be really messy. That was why she wanted to paint the sky, with lovely big fluffy clouds floating along. But each time she tried Tom laughed at her. 'You can't reach,' he said. 'You're too small.' And he leaned over her head, and did the bit she wanted to do.

At break she found someone had put her jacket on one of the higher pegs she could not reach, and she wouldn't ask Tom or anyone else to get it down. So she went outside without it, and felt cold. Then the playground helper told her off for not wearing a coat.

''I couldn't reach it," said Kitty, in a small voice.

"Oh, you're such a *dear little* thing," said the lady, nicely.

Kitty sighed. It really was not fair.

Bel Mooney

The Worst Witch

Miss Cackle's Academy for Witches stood at the top of a high mountain surrounded by a pine forest. It looked more like a prison than a school, with its gloomy grey walls and turrets. Sometimes you could see the pupils on their broomsticks flitting like bats above the playground wall, but usually the place was half hidden in mist, so that if you glanced up at the mountain you would probably not notice the building was there at all.

Everything about the school was dark and shadowy: long, narrow corridors and winding staircases – and of course the girls themselves, dressed in black gymslips, black stockings, black hob-nailed boots, grey shirts and black-and grey ties. Even their summer dresses were black-and-grey checked. The only touches of colour were the sashes round their gymslips – a different colour for each house – and the school badge, which was a black cat sitting on a yellow moon. For special occasions, such as prize-giving or Hallowe'en, there was another uniform consisting of a long robe worn with a tall, pointed hat, but as these were black too, it didn't really make much of a change.

Jill Murphy

Grace and Family

Extract 1

Grace and Nana left for Africa on a very cold grey day. They arrived in The Gambia in golden sunshine like the hottest summer back home. It had been a long, long journey. Grace barely noticed the strange sights and sounds that greeted her. She was thinking of Papa.

"I wonder if he will still love me?" thought Grace. "He has other children now and in stories it's always the youngest that is the favourite." She held on tightly to Nana.

Outside the airport was a man who looked a little like Papa's photo. He swung Grace up in his arms and held her close. Grace buried her nose in his shirt and thought, "I do remember."

In the car she started to notice how different everything seemed. There were sheep wandering along the roadside and people selling watermelons under the trees.

Extract 2

Next day, they went to the food market. It was much more exciting than shopping at home. Even the money had crocodiles on it! Lots of the women carried their shopping on their heads.

Then they went to a stall which was like stepping inside a rainbow. There was cloth with crocodiles and elephants on it and cloth with patterns made from pebbles and shells. And so many colours!

Mary Hoffman

Freedom for Prometheus

Even the gods grow wiser as they grow older. Almighty Zeus, king of the gods, looked down one day from Mount Olympus and saw Prometheus still chained to his rock, condemned for ever to be tortured by eagles. Zeus felt a kind of shame, because it is shameful for the strong to bully the weak.

And he felt a kind of pity, because it is sad to see a father kept from his children, an artist kept from his handiwork.

And he felt a kind of admiration: not just for Prometheus for enduring his pain, but for the little men and women Prometheus had made out of water and mud. If he had not given them the gift of fire, how could there be fires burning now on a thousand altars throughout the world, raising up holy, sweet-scented smoke to heaven?

For all they were cheeky and ugly and caught cold and grew old and stole and quarrelled and made mistakes and died, there were heroes and heroines among those men and women.

So Zeus broke Prometheus' chains with pliers of lightning, and wrapped the eagles in whirlwinds and spun them away to the four corners of the world. And Prometheus was free once more to champion the little people of the world, whom he had made out of water and mud.

Geraldine McCaughrean

50 LITERACY HOURS FOR LESS-ABLE
LEARNERS : Ages 7 to 9

SCHOLASTIC

The Fox and the Grapes

One day, a wandering fox noticed a bunch of grapes hanging down from a vine high above his head. They looked very juicy and tasty to the fox. He reached up tall on his hind legs but he couldn't reach them. Then he tried leaping in the air, snapping his teeth at the grapes, but still he couldn't quite reach them. After many unsuccessful and tiring leaps he stood under the grapes and decided to give up.

As he trotted off, he thought to himself, "Well, I didn't want those grapes anyway. I'm sure they were sour."

Moral

People often console or fool themselves after failure by pretending that they didn't ever want something the find they can't have.

The Tortoise and the Hare

A tortoise and a hare challenged each other to a race. At the start of the race, the hare set off at speed. Poor tortoise had hardly got going when hare bounded off into the distance. Noticing he was well ahead and out of sight, the hare slowed down and leant against a shady tree. "I don't need to run," he said to himself. "I could walk from here and still beat that tortoise, and I might as well have a little rest." So he settled himself against the tree trunk, and dozed off. While he was sleeping, the tortoise plodded steadily past. Tortoise carried on, determined, and by the time hare had woken up, tortoise was just crossing the winning line.

Moral

Success comes from focus and effort; pride and laziness bring failure.

The Froggy Princess

A long time ago, when there were dragons and wicked witches and knights in armour and fairy tales were true, there lived a beautiful princess called Princess Amanda.

I said she was beautiful. Well, she was beautiful when she wasn't crying. But she was always crying. Her nose was always red from crying, and her eyes were puffy and pink from crying.

Why did she cry so much? Because she was waiting for a handsome Prince to come to the castle and marry her. But no Prince ever came. Not one.

One fine summer day, Princess Amanda cried harder than she had ever cried before. She wept *buckets*. She cried so much and for so long that the tall, narrow turret in which she lived began to fill with water. It was when the water had risen just above her knees that she saw the frog. The frog was swimming in the water with its back legs going Per-chung, Per-chung. Its bright round eyes stared straight at her.

"Go away!" said the Princess. "I hate frogs! All slippery and slimy! Ugh!"

The frog said, "Qu-arckk." Then, "Don't be rude."

"What did you say?" said Princess Amanda who was so surprised by the talking frog that she forgot to cry. "*What?*"

The frog hopped out of the water and onto the Princess's lap.

Nicholas Fisk

Fantastic Mr Fox

Mr Fox crept up the dark tunnel to the mouth of his hole. He poked his long handsome face out into the night air and sniffed once.

He moved an inch or two forward and stopped.

He sniffed again. He was always especially careful when coming out from his hole.

He inched forward a little more. The front half of his body was now in the open.

His black nose twitched from side to side, sniffing and sniffing for the scent of danger. He found none, and he was just about to go trotting forward into the wood when he heard or thought he heard a tiny noise, a soft rustling sound, as thought someone had moved a foot ever so gently through a patch of dry leaves.

Mr Fox flattened his body against the ground and lay very still, his ears pricked. He waited a long time, but he heard nothing more.

'It must have been a field-mouse,' he told himself, 'or some other small animal.'

He crept a little further out of the hole … then further still. He was almost right out in the open now. He took a last careful look around. The wood was murky and very still. Somewhere in the sky the moon was shining.

Just then, his sharp night-eyes caught a glint of something bright behind a tree not far away. It was a small silver speck of moonlight shining on a polished surface. Mr Fox lay still, watching it. What on earth was it? Now it was moving. It was coming up and up … *Great heavens! It was the barrel of a gun!* Quick as a whip, Mr Fox jumped back into his hole and at that same instant the entire wood seemed to explode around him. *Bang-bang! Bang-bang! Bang-bang!*

Roald Dahl

I Can't Find It!

It was Saturday – Kitty's favourite day. She was looking forward to playing in her room, and making a mess, and running in the garden, and … 'Now Kitty,' said Mum, 'It's Melissa's birthday party today. Had you forgotten?'

Kitty groaned out loud. Then she banged her mug on the table. Then she kicked the table leg. Then she folded her arms crossly and frowned.

Daniel laughed, as usual. 'Oh Kitty-witty, must look pretty,' he sang, ducking as she threw a crust across the table at his head.

Mum clapped her hands. 'That's quite enough,' she said sternly. 'It'll be very nice for you to go to your cousin's party.'

'At least I'll get a going-home bag,' said Kitty gloomily.

She remembered the last time Melissa had a party. Two hours before they had to leave Mum had put her in the bath, to scrub her clean – which took quite a long time. She had washed Kitty's hair and tied it back with two blue ribbons. Ribbons! In Kitty's hair! Then she had made Kitty put on the brand new pretty dress she had bought specially. It was pale blue with lots of little white flowers all over it, and a white lace collar and cuffs. Clean white shoes and socks finished Kitty's party clothes.

Bel Mooney

George's Marvellous Medicine

He was especially tired of having to live in the same house as that grizzly old grunion of a Grandma. Looking after her all by himself was hardly the most exciting way to spend a Saturday morning.

'You can make a nice cup of tea for a start,' Grandma said to George. 'That'll keep you out of mischief for a few minutes.'

'Yes, Grandma,' said George.

George couldn't help disliking Grandma. She was a selfish grumpy old woman. She had pale brown teeth and a small puckered up mouth like a dog's bottom.

'How much sugar in your tea today, Grandma?' George asked her.

'One spoon,' she said. 'And no milk.'

Most grandmothers are lovely, kind, helpful old ladies, but not this one. She spent all day and every day sitting in her chair by the window, and she was always complaining, grousing, grouching, grumbling, griping about something or other. Never once, even on her best days, had she smiled at George and said, 'Well, how are you this morning, George?' or 'Why don't you and I have a game of Snakes and Ladders?' or 'How was school today?' She didn't seem to care about other people, only about herself. She was a miserable old grouch.

Roald Dahl

George Speaks

Laura's baby brother George was four weeks old when it happened. Laura, who was seven, had very much wanted a brother or sister for a long time. It would be so nice to have someone to play with, she thought. But when George was born, she wasn't so sure.

Everybody – her mother and father, the grandparents, uncles, aunts, friends – made such a fuss of him. And all of them said how beautiful he was. Laura didn't think he was. How could anyone with a round red face and a squashy nose and little tiny eyes all sunken in fat be called beautiful? She looked at him as he lay asleep in his carry-cot.

'Don't wake George up, will you?' her mother had said. 'I'll be in the kitchen if you want me.'

'I won't wake you,' Laura said to the sleeping baby. 'And I don't want to sound rude. But I must tell you something. You look just like a little pig.'

And that was when it happened.

The baby opened his eyes and stared straight at her.

'Pig yourself,' he said.

Laura gasped. A shiver ran up her spine and her toes tingled.

'What did you say?' she whispered.

'I said "Pig yourself",' said George. 'You're not deaf are you?'

'No,' said Laura. 'No, it's just that I didn't expect you to say anything.'

'Why not?'

'Well, babies don't say proper words. They only make noises, like Goo-goo or Blur-blur or Wah.'

Dick King-Smith

50 LITERACY HOURS FOR LESS-ABLE
LEARNERS : Ages 7 to 9

The Wrong Bag

SCENE ONE: Inside the front door of Darren's house. Mum answering door to Sally.

MUM: Hurry up Darren! You'll be late for school. Sally's here.

DARREN: Coming Mum! I forgot my football kit. .

DARREN comes to front door carrying his school bag.

DARREN: Hi Sal.

SALLY: Hi Daz.

MUM: Have you got the cakes we made for your class cake stall?

SALLY: I've got mine *(tapping her bag)*. They're really heavy.

DARREN looks in his bag.

DARREN: Oh no! Where are they?

MUM: In the kitchen, on the work surface.

Exit DARREN

MUM: He'd forget his head if it wasn't screwed on! *(MUM and SALLY laugh)*

SALLY: Boys! *(MUM and SALLY shake their heads.)*

DARREN comes back, out of breath.

DARREN: OK! Got them!

MUM: Don't be late home after football. Remember, it's Gran's surprise birthday party and you have to help me ice the cake we made for her last night. See you later!

Exit DARREN and SALLY. MUM waves.

END OF SCENE ONE

SCENE TWO: Year 3 classroom. The cake stall is all set up. The children enter. MR HARPER, the teacher is standing at the front.

MR HARPER: Well done all of you. What a lot of cakes!

GEMMA: We thought you might have eaten them all Mr Harper. We know you like cream buns!

MR HARPER Thank you Gemma! If I wasn't on a diet, this is the one I'd really fancy! *(holding a birthday cake)*

DARREN (TO SALLY): Oh no! That's my Gran's! I must have picked up the wrong bag! What am I going to do?

Campbell Perry

Calligrams

THE SHAPE I'M IN

Come and see the shape I'm in

Tall as a tale

Thin as a pin

 **w i d e** as a smile

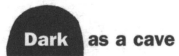 **Bright** --- as a tin

Dark as a cave

Curved as a wave

Wild as the rain

strong as a train

I'm *this* and that

I'm here   I'm there

eveRything

&

eveRywhere!

James Carter

Rhyming poems (1)

True Confession

On my birthday I wrapped
a big slice of chocolate cake
in pink paper to give
to Miss Twiglington,

but when I got to school
she was horrible to me;
'You haven't worked hard enough,
your spellings are bad

margin crooked,
fingerprints all over'
then she ripped out the page
and made me start again. I thought

'She's not getting that cake.'
When break time came
I ate it myself in the playground
and I didn't care.

Irene Rawnsley

The Magic Seeds

There was an old woman who sowed a corn seed,
And from it there sprouted a tall yellow weed.
She planted the seeds of the tall yellow flower,
And up sprang a blue one in less than an hour.
The seed of the blue one she sowed in a bed,
And up sprang a tall tree with blossoms of red.
And high in the tree-top there sang a white bird,
And his song was the sweetest that ever was heard.
The people they came from far and near,
The song of the little white bird to hear.

James Reeves

Rhyming poems (2)

The Town Child

I live in the town
In a street;
It is crowded with traffic
And feet;
There are buses and motors
And trams;
I wish there were meadows
And lambs.

The houses all wait
In a row,
There is smoke everywhere
That I go.
I don't like the noises
I hear—
I wish there were woods
Very near.

There is only one thing
That I love,
And that is the sky
Far above.
There is plenty of room
In the blue
For castles of clouds
And me, too!

Irene Thompson

The Country Child

My home is a house
Near a wood
(I'd live in a street
If I could!)
The lanes are so quiet,
Oh, dear!
I do wish that someone
Lived near.

There is no one to play with
At all.
The trees are so high
And so tall;
And I should be lonely
For hours,
Were it not for the birds
And the flowers.

I wish that I lived
In a town—
To see all the trams
Going down
A twinkling street
That is bright
With wonderful colours,
At night!

Irene Thompson

50 LITERACY HOURS FOR LESS-ABLE
LEARNERS : Ages 7 to 9

Water poems

There are Big Waves

There are big waves and little waves,
Green waves and blue,
Waves you can jump over,
Waves you dive through.

Waves that rise up
Like a great water wall,
Waves that swell softly
And don't break at all.

Waves that can whisper,
Waves that can roar,
And tiny waves that run at you
Running on the shore.

Eleanor Farjeon

After rain

Peach blossom after rain
Is deeper red;
The willow fresher green;
Twittering overhead;
And fallen petals lie wind-blown,
Unswept upon the courtyard stone.

Arthur Waley

Spring Rain

A good rain knows its season.
It comes at the edge of Spring.
It steals through the night on the breeze
Noiselessly wetting everything.
Dark night, the clouds black as the roads,
Only a light on a boat gleaming.
In the morning, thoroughly soaked with water,
The flowers hang their heavy heads.

Tu Fu, translated by Kenneth Rexroth

SCHOLASTIC

50 LITERACY HOURS FOR LESS-ABLE
LEARNERS : Ages 7 to 9